The Good Hope

The voyage of the *Good Hope* is a journey on which the life of the entire community depends. A storm rages, the women and children wait ashore, the boat follows the Greenland catch . . .

Lee Hall, writer of the award-winning *Billy Elliot* and *Spoonface Steinberg*, has relocated this Dutch classic of the social realist theatre to the Yorkshire fishing community of Whitby in 1900.

A poetic account of the fisherman's life, *The Good Hope* hasn't been performed in the UK for more than fifty years and is rediscovered at a time when the fishing industry is again in a time of struggle.

by the same author

Cooking with Elvis & Bollocks
Pinocchio
A Servant to Two Masters
Spoonface Steinberg

The Good Hope

by

Herman Heijermans

a new version by

Lee Hall

lyrics by **John Tams**

Methuen Drama

Methuen Drama

1 3 5 7 9 10 8 6 4 2

First published in 2001 by
Methuen Publishing Limited

Copyright © 2001 Lee Hall
Song Lyrics © 2001 John Tams

The author has asserted his moral rights

A CIP catalogue record for this book is available from the British
Library

ISBN 978-0-413-77165-0

Typeset by SX Composing DTP, Rayleigh, Essex
Printed and bound in Great Britain by
Cox & Wyman Ltd, Reading, Berkshire

Introduction

The Good Hope is one of those few plays that actually changed things. Heijermans wrote with such campaigning zeal about the deceit and corruption which allowed a fishing ship to go out in an unfit state that nine years later the Dutch actually passed an act that outlawed the practices which caused the play's central tragedy. So my problem was how to make a play that had so efficiently served its purpose speak with a freshness and urgency when everything appears to have changed.

The play is seemingly old-fashioned in its fiercely felt emotion and its unstinting quarry of injustice. But I quickly realised the key to understanding the work was to see how much Heijermans steers the play away from the melodrama of its time. A typical act of restraint is the central storm scene which is really just a conversation by a hearth but which vividly allows us to feel the enormity of what is happening to the men offstage. Heijermans creates a storm in the audience's mind rather than pursuing the spectacle that characterised popular theatre at the turn of the century. (Drury Lane, for instance, was famous for its earthquakes and shipwrecks at precisely this point.)

However, unlike other theatrical 'Realists' he resolutely chose to focus attention on the working classes. (Ibsen's *The Pillars of the Community* – almost identical in theme – opens in the shipowner's drawing room, for instance, whereas almost all of Heijermans' original play takes place in a fisherwoman's hovel.) *The Good Hope* is powerful as a piece of agitprop in direct proportion to its complexity at examining complicity and consensus. Heijermans' examination of the emotional and psychological economies at work in the community is just as acute as his sketches of the political and fiscal realities that underpin them. And it seems to me in this way *The Good Hope* is very much a precursor of Brecht's *Mother Courage* – another character who sends her sons to their doom but inspires pity as much as opprobrium.

So in the 'European Theatre' the play has gained an iconic status as a piece about resistance and the maintenance of dignity amidst the injustices of fate. In Truffaut's *The Last Metro*, as Catherine Deneuve nightly descends the cellar steps of her theatre to bring sustenance to her Jewish husband as he hides from the Nazis beneath the stage, it is no accident that she passes a poster for 'La Bonne Esperance'.

However, even knowing its history, I was still daunted about finding a contemporary relevance for a piece largely about outdated shipping laws in a small Dutch village at the turn of the last century. But within days of first reading the play a train was derailed at Hatfield and the emergent story of our railways seemed a sad, poetic repetition of the events of the play. Economic expediency had again lead directly to people's deaths. Then, as I embarked on the first draft, hospital workers in Dudley, striking over their concerns at PFI (Private Finance Initiative) in the Health Service, were writing to me for support. And it swiftly became clear that I did not have to worry about a contemporary resonance. In the 100 years since it was first written we are no further forward in solving the manifest problems that underlie the tragedy of *The Good Hope*. The issues about commerce and the common good, responsibility for our collective safety, and the public and private ownership of the fruits of our labour and the means by which we produce them are as contentious as ever.

But as much as the play is a powerful piece of political writing, throwing up many more questions than it answers, it is also a play about loss. The catastrophe of *The Good Hope* is always placed in the context of common mortality. Death, in the play, is inevitable and everyday but nevertheless this is a play of mourning. As we started rehearsals the World Trade Centre was destroyed and, as I am writing this, war-like reprisal seems imminent. I think everyone involved in the production feels the subject of mourning is about to gain an unfortunate pertinence, although none of us know exactly how.

The only thing for certain seems that the incremental progress people like Heijermans have gained in the past is not something we can rely upon for the future. The checks to tragedy, inequality or injustice are as fragile as ever and they must be vigilantly kept and fought for. I believe the strength of Heijermans' play is in its probing at the supposed consolations of compromise and spelling out the cost of the consensus politics the Makepeace character so eloquently elaborates. These problems are no less urgent because they are knotty. Although he is unequivocal about tracing the mechanisms of disaster he seems uneasy about 'working out' everything in the drama. His method is not didacticism, melodrama or agitprop. There is a cyclical pattern in the play which, although a concession to the strength of community to rejuvenate, is also a call to our conscience that here is a cycle as destructive as it is cohesive.

But even as a play of mourning it is still full of vibrancy, humour and life, although not of the sentimental kind. It is precisely the sentimental calls to community or to trite ideology to which the play raises its eyebrow. It is our everyday culpability that Heijermans is concerned most about. He sees it is in the small negotiations of common experience that our larger fate is sealed. It is in these small matters of course and conscience that he asks us to be most vigilant. As a character in the play points out, it is not death that is the problem; it is life we should be most worried about.

Lee Hall
September 2001

To Bill Bryden

The Good Hope

The Good Hope was first performed at the Cottesloe Theatre, Royal National Theatre, London, on 2 November 2001. The cast was as follows:

Kitty Fitzgerald, a fisherman's widow	Frances de la Tour
James, her son	Steve Nicolson
Ben, her younger son	Iain Robertson
Jo, her niece	Diane Beck
William, her older brother	John Normington
Christopher Makepeace, a shipowner	Tom Georgeson
Clementine, his daughter	Charlotte Emmerson
Arthur, his bookkeeper	Howard Ward
Simon, the drunken shipwright	John Tams
Mary, his daughter	Emma Bird
Michael, her fiancé	William Macbain
Dan, an old seaman	Trevor Ray
Susan, a fishwife	Linda Thompson
Sarah, a fisherman's widow	Sheila Reid
Harry, the barman of the Compass	Robert Oates
First Copper	Edward Clayton
Second Copper	Kenneth Anderson
Jed & **Trudger**, the village musicians	Alan Dunn & Graeme Taylor
Musicians	Christine Coe & Keith Thompson

Director Bill Bryden
Designer Hayden Griffin
Lighting Designer Rory Dempster
Music and lyrics John Tams
Sound Designer Ed Clarke

Act One

Whitby. 1900. A late blaze of summer. Rows of masts and sails blow in the gentle wind. The whole stage seems to move as if the audience were at sea, the winds whip up and blow harder, so the sails flap over one another. Through the forest of boats and the flap of canvas we glimpse a panorama of a thriving fishing port. All as if from the photographs of Frank Meadow Sutcliffe. The bustling quay fringed with stout Victorian rows of pubs, the Fisherman's Rest and the Compass, and shops, Braithwaite's General Store; and perched above it all the office of Makepeace Shipping. The stern line of buildings all intently focused on the quay, give way to the gentle incline of back gardens, which lead to the fishermen's cottages which ascend terrace after terrace up the steep banks of the town. At the very foot of the quay is a sandy beach where a few old rowing boats lie upturned, derelict among the old nets and detritus of the town. And leading offstage is the stone pier festooned with lobster nets and broken fish barrels. At every point in the play we are aware of the proximity of the sea. It is always lapping up to the action.

For the moment we catch only the vaguest glimpse of this panorama and the almost-dance to the hornpipe of the late summer breeze. Suddenly, they seem to have been blown together and somehow form an iris of a camera lens. The population of the town gather, facing the audience, as if posing for a group photograph. They sing.

I dreamed a dream the other night
Lowlands – Lowlands away, my John,
I dreamed a dream the other night
Lowlands away

I dreamed I saw my own true love
Lowlands – Lowlands away my John
Lowlands
       Away

I dreamed I saw my own true love
Lowlands away.

And as the song ends and there is a blinding flash, the company freezes, as if a camera has caught them.

The quayside.

As we get used to the light after the blinding flash, the people seem to disappear, fading away into history. On the stage, **Clementine***, the shipowner's daughter of a patronising but philanthropic bent, is adjusting an enormous camera on a tripod.* **William***, a once statuesque sea dog, now bent with old age, and his decrepit friend,* **Dan***, a sickly curmudgeon, are posing for the camera in a most unnatural manner.*

Clementine *adjusts the old men's poses and looks through the lens. A puff of smoke goes up as she takes a picture just as the old boys decide to adjust their position.* **Clementine** *is less than pleased.*

Clementine   Bugger.

She changes a plate, disgruntledly.

Can't you stand still?

William   I was standing still.

Clementine   You moved your leg.

William   What d'ya expect, it's gone to sleep.

Clementine   Now you've moved completely!

William   Well, it were a bloody ridiculous position int' first place.

Clementine   It is not a ridiculous position. It's picturesque.

William   I'd never stand like that.

Clementine   You just did.

William   Aye, cos I were put. I thought this were supposed to be 'real life'.

Dan *has steadfastly maintained his ridiculous pose. Still frozen, he moves his eyes to catch* **Clemetine**'s *attention.*

Dan Can I go yet?

Clementine Stay where you are.

She arranges **William**.

Just look over your shoulder – like so.

Dan I'll be late for tea, Miss.

Clementine Just be quiet.

Clementine *rearranges their poses.*

Dan Think I'm going to faint, Miss. You better hurry up or there'll be nowt left.

Clementine Right now, keep quite still.

Dan Why's he pulling that stupid face?

William What d'ya mean a stupid face?

Clementine Be quiet, the pair of you.

Dan I don't see the point in this posing around.

Clementine I'm just trying to capture a moment of truth.

Dan Look, truth is it's teatime.

Clementine You can't just photograph 'real life' willy nilly. Real life can be rather boring.

The two fishermen look at one another. It's the most natural pose they've made so far.

Don't move. That's perfect.

She fiddles with the camera.

Dan But Matron'll kill us if we're late. You don't know what it's like down there.

Clementine Well, at least somebody's got you two in check. Anyway, if I was in your shoes I'd thank God I was provided for in my old age.

Dan   I thank nobody, God included. I've served me time on deep water. I was a deckie when I was twelve years of age. I shouldn't have to put up with the bloody Matron. If I was a bit taller I'd bite the bugger's nose off.

Clementine   You're not in the 'Sailor's Rest' now, Daniel.

Dan   More's the pity. They'll've closed the bugger down at this rate. She threw me out last week. Just cos I were sick ont' floor. Tweren't my fault. Banned for three days. Had to sleep on the quay – in my condition. Wish I'd been finished by sharks years ago.

William   What shark's gonna touch you?

Clementine *laughs.*

Dan   You might laugh – I saw George Braithwaite bit clean in half and he were nowt but bag o' bones.

Clementine   A shark? In the North Sea?

Dan   *Six* of the buggers. Sea boiled beetroot.

Clementine   I wish I'd seen something really shocking like that. Did he scream?

Dan   No, just took his cap off and waved at Skipper.

William   Of course he screamed. You'd scream with a shark's set in your arse.

The sound of music starts to drift on to the stage – 'Clara's Waltz' from two itinerant musicians.

Clementine   The light's gone. Forget it. We'll try again tomorrow.

William   Thank Christ for that, I'm stiff as a parson's elbow.

Then **Jed** *and* **Trudger**, *the itinerant musicians, emerge from over a bank.* **Jed** *leads* **Trudger**, *blind as a bat, in an eccentric progress.* **Trudger** *is a fully kitted one-man band,* **Jed** *plays the banjo.*

Dan   Look, bugger off. You know we've got nowt to gi' ye.

William   Aye, away with you. We've been doing 'real life'. You want to try it some time.

Clementine   Don't be cruel. Here.

Clementine *throws a penny at them. It misses the bag on* **Trudger**'s *accordion and rolls away off the end of the quay and on to the beach.*

Dan   Charming. We've stood here for past half-hour and now she's throwing money at this lot.

Jed *immediately stops playing and climbs down on to the beach to find the penny. As he is tied to* **Trudger** *this causes havoc.* **Trudger** *exclaims as he is pulled about. Tangled chaos. They both fall on to the beach.*

The beach.

Dan   It's behind you.

More chaos.

William   Here.

They all struggle to find the penny.

Dan   Christ, you've buried it, you daft git.

Dan *and* **William**'s *assistance only adds to the tangle. They are all scrabbling on the ground. The inadvertent music of the one-man band adding to the chaos.*

Dan (*to* **Clementine**)   You and your grand ideas of charity.

As the hopeless crew attempt to discover the penny a lone figure ambles along the beach with a few meagre scraps of driftwood. **Ben** *is in his late teens, frail with a sensitive demeanour. He looks at the chaotic scrabbling with wry amusement.*

Clementine   Look, it has to be somewhere.

Ben joins the group and whispers into **Clementine***'s ear. He speaks with a pronounced stutter . . .*

Ben   M- m- maybes you should give 'em another one. I'm sure you can stretch to a p- p- penny.

Clementine   It was a ha'penny, actually.

Jed   A ha'penny!?

He considers giving up, but then thinks better of it.

Ben (*to* **Clementine**)   Christsake, just p- pretend you've f- found it.

Clementine *smiles at* **Ben**.

Clementine   Oh. Here it is.

She puts it in **Trudger***'s bag.*

William   And count yourselves lucky.

Jed *and* **Trudger** *go off, noisily.*

Ben   Best not t- throw money about in future. They'll only drink it.

William   Hark at him. You'd best think about earning yerself a crust than worrying 'bout t' other folks' welfare.

Ben   D . . . d . . . don't start.

William   Oh, you've got a gob as wide as t' Humber when it suits – but it's tight as a skate's arse when work's mentioned. The big man, eh? Least I don't shit me pants every time I see a trawler.

Dan   Come on, get us teas.

Clementine   Ten o'clock sharp, tomorrow.

Dan   We can't, Miss Makepeace. We're scrubbing stones int' morning.

Clementine   What's this? Another ancient custom?

Dan   That's right. Called cleaning the steps of the Seaman's Mission.

Clementine   Well, it'll have to be the afternoon.

William   So be it. We'll be here. See you, Miss. Ta-ta, Shite Pants.

William *and* **Dan** *go off.*

Clementine   He's got a sophisticated sense of humour, your uncle.

She dismantles the camera. **Ben** *says nothing.*

See you've been beachcombing.

Ben *nods.*

Clementine   Find much?

Ben   N- not much, twere neap tide – what we need's a storm. I found this, though . . .

He gives **Clementine** *a heart-shaped stone.*

Weird, in't it? Turn it round. It's a heart.

Clementine   It's quite beautiful. You're not really scared to go to sea, are you? Everybody does it.

Ben   Aye, but not everybody comes back.

Ben *helps* **Clementine** *with the camera and tripod.*

Clementine   So you are scared.

Ben   No. I just have a preference for d- d- dry land.

Clementine   How old are you?

Ben   Old enough.

Clementine   Really. I thought a strong lad like you'd be off in the Navy or something.

Ben   I were r- rejected.

Clementine   Why's that then?

Ben   I . . . I . . . I . . . I don't know, Miss . . .

Clementine   Maybe they took you for a coward. You're not scared of me, by any chance, are you?

Ben   I'm not scared of anything on dry land. I'd stick one in anybody if I had to.

Clementine   Are you sure about that?

Ben   No offence, Miss.

Clementine *sits on one of the upturned boats,* **Ben** *sits down next to her.*

Clementine   Don't worry. I don't scare that easily. Is your brother still in jail?

Ben   What's it to y- you?

Clementine   I expect you're ashamed of him. Getting done for insubordination. A bit too red-blooded for your liking?

Ben   W . . . what do you mean by that?

Clementine   Or maybe there's more to you than meets the eye?

She looks at him closely.

No, you're not the type to take advantage, are you?

Ben *stumbles over his answer.*

Ben   Y- you never know.

Clementine *is lying against the boat. She looks at* **Ben**. **Ben** *hesitates. She enjoys his discomfort.*

Clementine   Prove it?

Ben *might be about to make a move, when . . .*

Backyard of house.

There is a shout from inside the house (offstage).

Kitty (*off*)   Benjamin! Benjamin!

A chicken flies out of the door and into the yard.

What the hell's going on here?

Kitty, *a stately but harried fisherwoman in her fifties, bursts through the door into the back garden of her cottage. The weight of her experience has done nothing to diminish her vigour. She immediately begins to give chase to the chicken.*

Kitty   Benjamin!!

Ben *looks up to the yard where* **Kitty** *is running around.*

Ben   S . . . s . . . shit.

Ben *looks at* **Clementine** *apologetically, scrambles up the bank and climbs over the fence to* **Kitty**.

Kitty   How the hell did they get out?

They both chase chickens.

Ben   It's not end of w- w- world, Mam.

Kitty   It was in the bloody stewpot, you daft bloater. The sooner I'm shot of you the better.

She plonks a chicken into his hands.

Ben   H- h- honest, Mam . . . I . . .

Suddenly, **Jo**'s *head appears from a trench in the garden.* **Jo** *is an unsentimental but intensely warm young woman in her twenties. She has a wit and vital directness that give her an edge of sexual danger. She is covered from head to toe in mud.*

Jo   For Christsakes, Kitty. I let them out myself.

Kitty   What the hell did you do that for?

Jo   I couldn't stand the bloody clamour of them cooped up all day.

Kitty   So you'd sooner they were plodging int' stew.

Jo   Listen, I'm t' one stuck down here digging the spuds out while you two are swanning . . .

Kitty   I've been working all morning.

Jo   What about Captain Cook, then?

Ben   I've b- been collecting driftwood.

Jo   I'll give you driftwood straight up your arse. Scared of the spuds, 'nall, are you?

Ben   Oh, s . . . s . . . shut up.

Jo   Look at this one. Aaaaagghghg!!??

She throws a potato at **Ben** *as if it were some terrifying beast. She points to it on the ground.*

(*Mock horror.*) Look out! Look out. It's c- c- c- coming for you. Oh my God, you're surrounded by vegetables.

Ben   B- b- b- GET LOST, will yous.

Ben *storms off.* **Jo** *and* **Kitty** *laugh, then they spot* **Clementine** *looking over the fence.*

Kitty   Oh, good afternoon, Miss.

Clementine   He's a little sensitive.

Kitty   He's a little layabout. Can I help you, Miss?

Clementine   He dropped this.

Clementine *gives her the heart-shaped stone.*

Jo   He wants it chucking at him. I've been up since the crack of dawn and he's been pissing about collecting pebbles. Look at this lot, they're rotten.

Kitty   It's all the bloody rain. This is the first fine day we've had all week. Oh, the lot of the poor, Miss. God knows how we're going to get through winter if it keeps going like this.

Jo   Here we go – the Lamentations! Look on the bright side for once in your life. Least James'll be back.

Kitty   What good's that gonna do?

Jo   You might just break into a smile for five minutes. Look, I caught a rabbit.

Jo brings a rabbit from her trench.

Clementine   Were you poaching?

Jo   Poaching? No, it had a taste for manky spuds – so I brayed it with t' spade. Worth a tanner, I reckon.

Clementine   I say, well aimed. Anyway, tell Ben I'll be on the quay in the morning. I best be going.

She turns to go but at the door is **Mr Makepeace**, *the shipowner. He has the charm and confidence that affluence makes easy, but there is a rough edge which tells us it was hard won. He stands with a chicken in his hands.*

Makepeace   Afternoon. (*To* **Kitty**.) I think this might be yours.

Kitty   Oh my goodness, Mr Makepeace.

Makepeace (*to* **Clementine**)   I thought I might find you here. (*Of the chicken.*) It was in the front room.

The chicken shits on **Makepeace**'s *jacket.*

Kitty   I'm so sorry about the chicken, sir.

Kitty *fusses over him.*

Makepeace   Don't worry about that, Kit, a little muck never hurt anybody. Hello there.

Jo   Hello.

Kitty   You remember Jo, sir, my niece.

Jo   I won't . . . er . . . [shake your hand].

She shows her filthy hands in explanation.

Makepeace   Going somewhere posh, are you?

Jo .   A tea dance int' Scarborough.

Makepeace   A proper cheeky piccaninny? (*To*
Clementine.) Well, come on, sweetheart, take me picture.
'The Shipowner visits the Cottages.'

Clementine   Certainly not.

Makepeace   Oh go on. (*To* **Jo**.) Come over here. They'll
think I was in darkest Africa.

Clementine   Shut up, Father. You don't know anything
about photography.

Makepeace   Oh, that's very nice, in't it. You spend a
fortune ont' camera and she won't even take your own
picture.

Clementine   I don't find you an interesting subject,
Father.

Makepeace   Two years at boarding school and she thinks
she's Lady Muck. You'll end up like your mother.

Ben *comes in and stops dead when he sees* **Makepeace**.

Makepeace   Ah, little Benjamin – just the fella.

Ben   M- m- me, sir?

Makepeace   The one and only. How long have you been
out o' work, son?

Ben   Nine month.

Kitty   You little sod. More than a year, sir.

Ben   N- n- no it's not . . .

Jo   What are you? Stupid as well as lily-livered.

Makepeace   All right, all right, children. Now then, Benji
– what would you say to forty-seven?

Ben   Forty-seven, sir?

Makepeace   The *Good Hope*.

Clementine   The *Good Hope*?

Makepeace   You keep out of this.

Clementine   But . . .

Makepeace   I've warned you. I'm in the middle of a business arrangement here. Now bugger off home.

Clementine   Do you realise how vulgar you are, Father?

Makepeace   Thank you, Clementine. I'll see you at home.

Makepeace *looks sternly at* **Clementine** *and she, reluctantly, leaves.*

Makepeace   I've got a fleet of eight luggers on my mind. You didn't think I had time for compliments, did you? Anyway, what about it, son?

They all look at **Ben**.

Kitty   Say something.

Ben   I- I- I'd rather . . .

Kitty   'Rather'!

Makepeace   Now, now, children. It's up to you. She was only out four times last year and made four thousand. She's just been int' dock, fully insured, Adams is skipper, we're looking for a deckie. Take it or leave it, son.

Ben   I- I- I- I . . .

Jo   For Christsake, get it out.

Ben   I . . . don't know, sir.

Kitty   You obstinate little shit. I should drag you on by the scruff of your neck.

Makepeace   What's up, little man? You've got one trip behind you?

Ben   Just a day trip, sir. As cabin boy.

Jo (*with contempt*)   You don't understand. He don't like the sea, sir.

Makepeace   Do you think anyone likes it? I used to go with your grandfather when we were half your age – oh yes, I'd've rather been tied to me mammy's apron sooner than stood out with fists like clods of ice – I'd've rather been home wi' a nice warm plate of soup rather than biting the heads off mackerel. But that's not how things work, son. Is it? What would your father say?

Ben   My father drowned, sir. And my brother Joseph and my brother Henry, sir. I just c- can't, sir.

Makepeace   Fine. If that's how you want it. No one's trying to force you. Sorry, Kit. I sympathise, son. My dad didn't die in his bed neither. But if we were all as sentimental as you, we'd be living off seaweed and field mice.

Kitty   I could tan your hide for you.

Makepeace   Whoa, calm down, lass. Can't catch a herring with a pitchfork.

Jo   Give me a pitchfork and I'll sort the bugger out.

Makepeace   You'll get more from a trout if you tickle its tummy.

Kitty   What are you trying to say, anyway? That *I've* forgotten. How dare you even bring up their names. Have you any idea what I went through?

Kitty *breaks down.*

Jo   You see.

Makepeace   Come on, Kitty.

Kitty   Twelve year next month.

Makepeace   I know. It was September eighty-eight.

Kitty   He were only six. You can't even remember them.

Ben   It's not my f- f- fault.

Makepeace   Well, what are you getting yourself worked up for?

Ben   I just want a different t- trade.

Makepeace   What were you thinking of? You can't read or write.

Ben   I'll do anything, sir. I'll d- dig, plant things, s- s- salt down, anything. I'll be a b- bricklayer, a carpenter . . .

Jo   Or Lord Mayor. Or the bloody Chief Constable. You could crawl around at night arresting smugglers.

Ben   I- I don't care what you say. Did I come c- crying when the salt cracked me hand open . . .

Kitty   What makes you think you'd be any better off as a brickie. They're dropping off ladders left right and centre.

Makepeace   She's right. Do you think you'd be any safer down a mine? Or in a factory? Do you think you're going to be safe racing round in a train? Accidents happen. It's a fact of life, son. You might walk out of here and get run down by a pony and trap.

Kitty   We haven't got a choice, Ben. God knows what winter'll bring, potatoes are rotten already.

Makepeace   All over Yorkshire.

Ben   I- I- I just can't, sir.

Kitty   Well, get out.

Ben   P- p- please, Mam.

Kitty (*with real anger*)   Now!

Makepeace   Kitty . . .

Ben *looks at his mother, turns and leaves.*

Makepeace   I suppose that's a no, then.

Jo   I'll talk to him. It's a good job James isn't here. He'd murder the little sod.

Jo *goes out.*

Makepeace   James. Six months, wasn't it?

Kitty   That's right.

Makepeace   Insubordination?

Kitty   He's fiery b' nature, sir.

Makepeace   He's a fool.

Kitty   He was provoked, sir.

Makepeace   Nobody 'provokes' in the Navy. If there weren't discipline the officers'd be shark bait.

Kitty   But . . .

Makepeace   And she's got her eye on him, I take it.

Kitty   He's a good-looking lad.

Makepeace   He's from a handsome family, Kitty.

Kitty   He's a decent man, sir. Been to India twice. He's just proud. God knows what he'll do when he gets out. I'll have to put him up here. It's a waste, sir – a strong lad like him.

Makepeace   He's a Red Flagger, Kitty.

Kitty   But he's known the sea since . . .

Makepeace   Forget it, Kit. I can't take a bloody red on. All the same those lads from the Navy.

Kitty   But you don't understand . . .

Makepeace   Look, I'll not have anyone trying to steal me bloody boats off me. I worked my way up from nowt. You know what I put into this. What's wrong with that? I keep half of Whitby in a job. Am I unfair, Kitty? Tell me, am I unfair with anybody?

Kitty No.

Makepeace *and* **Kitty** *look at each other. We sense there is a long, unrequited history there.*

Makepeace Tell him to keep his gob shut and I'll send him out on the *Hope*.

Kitty You're a good man, Christopher.

Makepeace It's just business. He knows how it works.

Kitty Will I tell him to go to the docks or your office?

Makepeace Just tell him one word of socialism and he'll never work again. Understand?

Kitty Yes, sir.

There is the sound of a trawler whistle. Suddenly, **Susan**, *an older woman full of hope and compassion, bursts through the back door of an adjacent cottage and runs into her garden.*

Susan Kitty, d'ye hear? Great news. It's the *Anna*.

Susan *does not stop and runs from her garden down to the quay and off along the pier.* **Kitty** *and* **Makepeace** *immediately rush to catch sight of the boat returning.* **Kitty**'s *expectant look suddenly grows grim with trepidation.*

Makepeace She's flying a black flag.

Kitty A death on board.

Makepeace Not another crewman. This is a blow. I best go down.

Kitty I'll come with you.

Kitty *and* **Makepeace** *follow* **Susan** *down the bank with urgency. Other people run along the quay in the direction of the ship, and soon disappear offstage.*

The stage is bare, then centre stage a figure appears carrying a meagre bundle. **James**, **Kitty**'s *son, is in his early twenties, normally rugged, handsome and self-possessed. But when we look closer we see he* *is filthy and haggard. There is a frailty under his pride and swagger that tells us every movement is fought against great pain. He emerges into the street which leads to* **Kitty***'s garden. He is perplexed that no one is around. He makes his way, with some effort, to the garden. As no one is there he climbs over the fence and looks through the doorway to the inside of the cottage.*

James (*shouting*)   Mam?

He comes out. He starts to walk down towards the quay. **Ben** *is coming up the other way. He stops and stares in disbelief.*

James   I don't bite, you know.

Ben *runs up the bank and hugs him.*

Ben   J- James.

James   Where's Mam?

Ben   I d- d- don't know, she . . .

James   What's the matter with you?

Ben   N- nowt . . .

James   What do you mean nowt?

Ben   You look . . . pale.

James   What did ya expect. A suntan?

Ben   I hardly recognised you.

They sit in the garden.

James   Is there owt to drink?

Ben   I d- d- don't think so.

James   Well, go and bloody fetch summat.

Ben   I haven't got any money.

James   For Christsakes.

He throws **Ben** *some money.*

Ben   Where did you get that?

James   It's got bugger all to do with you. Just get uz summat to eat, will you.

He calls after **Ben**.

Benny. Is she all right? Me mam?

Ben *doesn't reply*.

James   And Jo? Is she angry?

Ben   W- w- what about?

James   Don't be a twat, Benny.

Ben   I'm just . . . I'm a bit surprised. I don't know.

James   Piss off out of it, will you.

Ben *slips out. We hear* **Jo** *singing*.

Jo
　　If I had the wings of Noah's dove
　　Jimmy where are you bound to
　　I'd fly back home to the one I love
　　Across the Western Ocean

She appears, carrying the dead rabbit. She sees **James** *and drops it. She flies over to him and kisses him – then bursts into tears.*

James   Stop it! Stop howling.

Jo   Jim. Jim.

James   Come on. Shush. Stop crying now.

Jo   I can't help it, Jim.

James   Get off. You'll smother uz. Just give uz a bit of space.

Jo *backs off*.

Jo   What happened to your beard?

James   Confiscated by Her Majesty. Apparently she took a liking to it. What do you reckon?

Jo You look great.

James I look like shit.

Jo No. Not to me, Jim.

James I'm *fucked*, Jo. Look at uz.

Jo No, James.

James I've been lying in me own shit for six months.

Jo *is crying.* **James** *gives her no comfort.*

James What did you expect?

Ben *comes back. He approaches* **James** *tentatively.*

Ben Some of Harry's gin.

Jo That moonshine!

Ben For him.

Jo Ben . . .

James Mind your own business, will you. Get a glass. Sod it.

He drinks the gin from the bottle.

That's better. What's the time?

Ben Half four.

Jo Please. Eat some bread, won't you?

Jo *starts to go inside,* **James** *stops her.*

James I don't want bread. Can't keep anything down.

He drinks some more gin and coughs.

Jo Please, James. That's enough, you can't take it.

James Enough! I haven't even started. (*He drinks more.*) There. (*And more.*) And another fathom. Yeah, that'll put a bit of colour in me cheeks. What's the matter? You never seen anyone drink before?

He drinks more. Coughs.

Where the hell did you get this?

He drinks some more. Burps.

Is there anything to eat?

Jo   Look. Caught it myself. It's not been dead an hour.

She shows him the rabbit.

James   It'll do for the morrow. Here, go and get some brawn or something.

James *throws* **Ben** *some money.*

Jo   What you doing? You can't go wasting that on cooked meat. I'll make you something . . .

James   Look, I've had nowt but gruel for six months, woman. If I want meat I'll have it. And get some cheese while you're on.

Ben *exits.* **James** *reaches for the bottle.*

Jo   Stop it, Jim. Stop it.

James *drinks too much. He coughs violently and retches.* **Jo** *takes the bottle off him. He spits out bile.*

Jo   Sit down, pet.

James   So who have you been going with since I've been inside then?

James *stares aggressively at* **Jo**. *She stares back through the insult.*

Jo   Who do you think? Uncle Willie and his mate, Dan.

James *stares at her angrily, then his face bursts into a smile.*

James   You daft hap'o'rth.

Jo *laughs.* **Kitty** *comes on from the quay and starts up the hill. She is obviously upset at the death. She relays the news with some urgency to* **Jo**.

Kitty   Jo. Jo. Terrible news. It's Susan's bloke, Stephen. He collapsed two days ago . . .

As **Kitty** *approaches the cottage she sees* **James** *and falls silent. They stare at one another.*

James   Mam.

Kitty   Jesus.

James   No. It's just me – James.

Kitty   Oh, you'll give me a bloody heart attack.

James   It'll take more than that to see *you* off.

James *goes to embrace her.*

Kitty   What the hell were you thinking of?

James   Oh, Jesus Christ, don't start, will you.

Kitty   Don't Jesus Christ me, young man.

James   I didn't come back to be got at.

Kitty   What did you expect, you ignorant sod?

James   What do you want me to do? Stand int' corner?

Kitty   The whole of t' harbour talking. I couldn't even go to t' quay without people . . .

James   Look, if anybody's got stuff to say they can say it to me face.

Kitty   So you can punch their lights out.

James   He deserved what he got, Mam.

Kitty   He was your skipper, bloody fool.

James   He was a bastard. I should have done him proper when I had the chance.

Kitty   Have you any idea what you've done to us, James?

She starts crying.

James   First they lock you up like a dog, then send you home to this!

He looks at **Kitty** *who is staring at him with immense anger and disappointment, tears streaming down her cheeks.*

Mam.

Jo   Kitty.

Kitty   Did you think once of your poor father?

James   Dad's dead, Mam.

Kitty   Have you any idea what he put up with?

James   Well, you should be glad that I won't let them kick me around.

Kitty   No. But you'll let them bang you up in jail.

James   If it happened again tomorrow, I'd still break his jaw for him.

Kitty   If *what* happened?

Jo   Sit yourself down, Jim, take it easy.

James   Take it easy? I've been sat on me arse for six months, for Christsake. So you just think I should just stand there like a lass while people slag off me family.

Jo   You've got thicker skin than that?

James   He called you a hoor.

Jo   A what!

James   You heard.

Jo   The bastard!!

Kitty   Language!

James   So I waited till graveyard watch and gave him 'good hiding. Sorted him out. 'Cept five minutes later I was straight down t' hatch. Six months in solitary. A ban for ten year.

Kitty   Why didn't you explain to the commanding officer? You can't go round calling people like that.

James   The commanding officer!?

Kitty   He could have sorted it out. There are rules.

James   And do you think they're made for us, Mam?

Kitty   If you'd've just gone to the captain for a quiet word.

James   Oh for Christsake, Mam. A quiet word! I was lucky they didn't have uz flogged. You don't think they locked uz up because I had a barney with the quartermaster? They locked uz up cos of *what I was reading.* Otherwise I'd still be swinging on me bunk in Bay of Biscay.

Kitty   What were you reading? Not that socialist rubbish?

James   It's not rubbish, Mam.

Kitty   I thought I brought you up decent.

James   Decent? So I could be treated like a slave. So I can spend my life licking some bloke's boots so he can toss his scraps at uz like a dog. Have you any idea what it's like in t' Navy?

Kitty   Of course I know what it's like.

James   I fought in a war, Mam. I stuck a knife in somebody's head. I stabbed a fella in the bloody heart. I killed people. I was a hero. Look at me now.

He takes off his shirt. We see in his face it is painful. His body is covered in scabs, sores and bruises. It is both shocking and disgusting. He stretches out his arms offering his wounds in some sort of supplication.

Look at me. That's what they does to uz heroes. A quiet word!?

Kitty *stares at him.*

Kitty   What have they done to you, son? I hardly recognise you.

James *stands in speechless anger.*

Kitty   Your anger, son.

James   I know – why should I be angry? Just because they took a bairn who couldn't read nor write and drilled the life out of him so he could barely stand up straight. Just so they made him cut other blokes into horse meat to save his own skin. Just to end up in a cell, lying in his own piss, sweating like a dying pig in his own shit and vomit . . .

Jo   Stop it. Stop it. Don't say any more.

He takes some more drink.

Kitty   James. James.

James   Let uz finish. Hallucinating. Shitting himself. Drinking water from a slop can. Screaming for dear life. Getting beaten for t' privilege. Just because I read a few pamphlets about the dignity of man. No, why the hell should I be angry?

Silence. **Jo** *approaches him.*

Jo   James.

Ben *stands looking at him.*

James   Anyway, let's not make a meal of it.

He holds back tears.

Have you got a light?

He puts his shirt back on. He tends to **Kitty**.

Now, come on, Mam. Take the weight off your feet. I see the chickens got out again.

Pause.

With a bit of luck I'll be out again in no time. Two days. That'd be all. Two days out and I'll be right as rain.

A bell starts to ring from the direction of the quay.

What's going on?

Kitty   It's the *Anna*. Brought back Stephen Kemp. Died yesturday. He'd been bad for a while.

James   Stephen Kemp. What the hell was he doing out at his age?

Kitty   You can't live ont' wind.

James   We should go down, Mam.

Kitty   Yes, we should go down, son, we should.

James *takes* **Kitty**'s *hand and they head off down the bank and along the quay, followed by* **Jo**.

Along the pier, **Dan** *appears with a rackety fish-cart on which a boy is wrapped in a shroud. The women of the town have gathered and, with great dignity, they bear the body off.*

As the body is carried back to the town the piped lament, which follows the procession, turns into a hornpipe and the stage transforms into the outside of The Compass.

Act Two

Dusk. Early autumn.

The set is almost a cross-section, cutting a line from the back of a huge quayside pub, on to the street which leads to the quay, which falls down into the harbour lined with the masts and sails of a myriad vessels. We are outside in the courtyard of the Compass. It is decked with lights and streamers for a party, there is a serving hatch and a cellar door. This leads to a covered alley which runs the whole length of the pub, and leads on to the cobbled street, lined with gas lamps, which in turn gives way to the quayside studded with moorings. The sails flap gently in the September breeze. The feel is of summer's very last night.

*The sun is setting and through the act, the light gradually fades to darkness. The courtyard is lit by the lamps decked out for **Kitty**'s party, and the quay by gas lamps, lit by an old lighter meandering along the harbour.*

Harry, *the barman, comes through the courtyard and drops an empty keg into the cellar and shuts the wooden hatch.*

Jed *and* **Trudger** *are tuning up whilst* **Kitty** *and* **Jo** *are fussing at a trestle table that contains their spread of food. Perhaps tying a sign wishing* **Ben** *farewell. However,* **Kitty** *sees something's missing . . .*

Kitty   Harry. Where are the pickled onions? I ordered pickled onions.

Harry   No one said owt to me about pickled onions.

Kitty   You have to have pickled onions. You can't eat all this potted meat without a pickled onion.

Jo   Anyway, they were paid for.

Harry   Look, nobody's paid for any onions pickled or otherwise to my knowledge. If they have I'll knock it off t' reckoning.

Kitty   I don't want it knocked off, I want me pickled onions.

Harry   Tough, I haven't got any pickled onions. Look, have a pint on the house, Kitty, and calm down.

Kitty   This would never happen in the Sailor's.

Harry   The Sailor's! You'd be lucky to get out alive, eating owt in there.

He presents two foaming pints of ale.

Here's to t' young un.

Simon *and* **Mary** *come along the quayside and down the alley to the party.* **Simon** *is rather the worse for wear.*

Mary   Helloooo!

Jo   Hello, Mary.

Mary *stops.*

Mary   There's no one here.

Jo   We're here!

Kitty   The lad's are upt' house getting ready.

Simon   I was told there were a party.

Harry   Simon.

Simon *ignores him and heads straight for the spread.*

Simon   What? No pickled onions.

Mary   Oh for God's sake, Dad, sit down.

Simon   Call this a party. I'm off to t' Sailor's.

Simon *leaves.*

Jo   One down . . .

Mary   Dad! Dad!

Simon *heads up the quay.*

Simon   Leave uz alone.

Mary   It's that way.

She indicates the correct way to the Sailor's Rest. **Simon** *proudly turns round without acknowledging* **Mary** *and heads off out of view.*

He's at it as soon as cock crows.

Jo   He's doing no harm.

Kitty (*to herself*)   It's a bloody disgrace. I'm going to Braithwaite's.

Jo *and* **Mary** *watch* **Kitty** *go off in a tizzy.*

Mary   Should've seen him yesturday. Came out of t' Sailor's – fell straight int' harbour. Took five of them to drag him out – then he was back in t' Sailor's suppin' brandy without even drying off. Me mam would've killed him. I don't know what to do. If he carries on at this rate, I'll have to stick a bloody cork down his neck.

Harry   What can I get you?

Mary (*to* **Harry**)   Pint of ale, lover. (*To* **Jo**.) When are they off, then?

Jo   Bout eight to catch tide. Anyways, did you get owt sorted with Michael?

Mary   Did I heck. Tried to wangle summat wi' magistrate. But soonest we can get t' licence is a fortnight, and he'll be ten mile off the Hook of Holland. We'll have to wait till he gets back. Jo, I'll be showing.

Jo   Ach, nobody'll notice. Not with your figure.

Mary   What's that supposed to mean?

Jo   James's agreed to December. Soon as he's back.

Mary (*screams*)   No.

Jo   Yes.

Mary   You as well! Come on, spill the beans then.

Jo   Shhh. Haven't told Kitty yet, she'll kill uz.

Enter **Kitty**, *with a huge jar of pickled onions.* **Jo** *shuts up.*

Kitty (*to* **Harry**)   Was that difficult? It's the last time I'm
booking here. Those pasties must be a week old. Onion,
anyone?

Jo   Stop fussing, Kitty, and sit down.

Kitty   Mary. Look what I've got for our Benji. What do
you think?

She holds up some earrings.

Jo   I still think you should give them to James.

Kitty   No, it's only fair. Now he's come to his senses.

Mary   Where did you buy them?

Kitty   Buy them. Do you think I'm made of money?
(*Pointedly to* **Harry**.) This spread just about ruined us. They
used to be Jack's.

Mary   Look, they've got little ships on them and
everything.

Jo   I still say James is t' one takes after his father. I tell you
what I'd give Benji, a good slapping.

Kitty   Leave the poor bugger alone for once in his life.
Fair dos. He took his time. But he signed, didn't he. I just
want to give him a proper send-off, after everything he went
through with Jack and everything.

Jo   Christ. One minute you're wanting to crucify him and
t' next he's up for t' sainthood.

Kitty   All right, all right. He might have been a little
bugger but let bygones be bygones. Never part in anger.
Come on, Mary, would you like a bit of beetroot? I'd get
stuck in before those greedy beggars get here.

William, *smoking a pipe, comes along the corridor with* **Dan**.

Kitty   Talk of the devil.

William   Three young lasses and not a single fella in sight.
Looks like we've come at right time, Dan.

William *surveys the sandwiches, takes a drag of his pipe and coughs — all over the spread.*

Kitty   And you can put that filthy pipe out. I'm not having you stinking the place out.

William   Great party this is gonna be.

Dan   We're not stopping . . . Oh, sandwiches!

Jo   So you'll not be wanting a drink then, Bill?

William   I'll write you out me will.

Jo   Dan?

Dan   Just a drop of brandy, love. Just to wet me whistle. Make that a double.

Kitty   Hey, I'm not made of money.

Harry *supplies the booze.*

William   Where's the lads, then?

He carefully knocks back the drink in one. **Dan** *is stuffing his face.*

Dan   Nice bit of pasty, is that?

Kitty   Would you like a onion?

Dan   No thanks, love. Doesn't agree.

Dan *continues to stuff his face as if food was going out of fashion. Then sits down, exhausted. He yawns.*

Mary   You're not sleepy already, are you?

Dan   I'm proper poorly. It's all that chewing.

Jo   There's beds upstairs. Get yoursel a lie-down.

Dan   No. I'll just have a nice sit by here.

William   He'd be up like a whippet if you went with him.

Jo   I think he'd be better off with hot-water bottle.

William   Well, I'm available.

Kitty   You! Matron has to help you on with your breeches.

William   Exactly – cos I'm irresistible.

Kitty   That's not what she told me about your breeches.

William   Unlike Matron, we fellas mature like a good wine.

Jo   An old cheese.

Enter **Sarah**.

Sarah   Cooee!

William   Hello, hello, me luck's in.

Sarah   Hello there, Danny. Hello there, Mary. Hello, Kitty, Jo . . .

William   How do?

Sarah *ignores him*.

Jo   Drink, Sair?

Sarah   No, not for me. Go on then, a small one.

Jo   Ale?

Sarah   Make it a pint. What a lovely spread.

Kitty   Pickled onion?

Sarah   Not for me. (*She is handed the drink.*) Bless you. To the lads . . . where are . . . ?

Kitty   They'll be down shortly. Ben's loading the oilskins with James. They're off at eight.

Sarah *has finished her pint*.

Sarah   Nice drop, that. Where were you the other day, Kitty? At Eileen's wedding?

Kitty   Was busy.

Sarah   Oh, very superior spread, proper bit of class.
Mind, the bride was bladdered, five gins, seven whiskies and
a quart of that Madeira.

William   I bet those sweet lips were sticky that night, eh,
Dan?

Dan *is asleep and wakes with a jolt.*

Dan (*muttering*)   No, Matron, not . . . Oh!

Kitty   Oh, leave him be. He only comes out for a nap.

William *gets his pipe out and starts to stuff it.*

Kitty   William.

Chastised, he puts it away. **Jed** *and* **Trudger** *arrive.*

Kitty   All right, lads.

Jed   We'll just set ourselves up over here [i.e., by the food].

He starts eating.

Kitty   Go steady on wi' those sandwiches. You're the
'turns'.

Jo   Will you take another, Sair?

Sarah   Oh no. I'm not stopping. Oh, go on then. One for
the road.

Kitty   Come on, you two. Sing for your supper.

Kitty *notices that* **Jed** *and* **Trudger** *(the band) are stuffing their
faces. She rushes over snatching a sandwich out of their hands.*

Kitty   Cut that out you two. Sing for your supper.

Jed *and* **Trudger** *start playing a hornpipe.* **Sarah** *starts dancing
and everyone claps her on. As the music gets wilder* **Michael** *runs up
the quay and grabs* **Mary**. *He spins her round high in the air, kissing
her with gusto and passion. Everyone cheers,* **Mary** *squeals with
exhilaration and delight.* **Michael** *reels her round and round, down
the alleyway, and he ends exhausted on the quay. In the courtyard, the
band are on to another hornpipe and there is less energetic dancing. By*

now the quay is in half light. **Michael** *kisses* **Mary**, *their hearts obviously pounding. As they snog they try to converse.*

Mary   You should be more careful. A lass in my condition.

Michael   I think you can take more than a bit of dancing.

Mary   It's all sorted for when ye get back. Maybe *we* could have a do in the Compass?

Michael   What with those sandwiches?

Mary   I'll be showing you know. I don't know what Dad'll say.

Michael   He'll be grateful you've not married some infertile.

Michael *smothers her with kisses. Suddenly,* **Simon** *staggers past them and dances into the pub, doing his own version of a hornpipe.*

Mary   Dad!

They follow him into the pub.

Storm (*drunk*)   Wey hey.

Simon's *increasingly energetic dance causes him to fall over. Everyone cheers.* **Michael** *picks him up.*

Michael   Come on, Big Man

He props him up against the wall.

Kitty   Hello Simon.

Simon *looks up at* **Kitty** *and burps loudly.*

Simon   Don't mind me.

William   Would you like a drop of ale, son?

Mary   No – he would not.

Simon   What do you mean – he would not?

Michael   He's not doing any harm.

Mary   You've had quite sufficient.

Simon   I haven't even started.

Kitty   Have you seen James, Simon?

Simon   James-Simon?

William   For Christsake, give him one for the gangplank.

Mary   No. No. Don't give him anything.

Simon   Hard lines. Carries his own supplies.

Simon *gets a little bottle out of his pocket and takes a swig.*

Sarah *finishes off her second pint, a prodigious feat.*

Sarah   Well, I best be off then.

Jo   Are you sure you don't want to wait? They'll be down any minute.

Sarah   I don't want to be an imposition. Maybe I'll have a little whisky and be on me way. (*To* **Harry**.) No, make that another pint, love.

James *arrives. A cheer.*

James   It's all hands on deck. Hello there, Si, not pissed again, are you, lad?

Simon   Haven't touched a drop.

Mary   Wait till you get home, Dad.

James   Oh, let the bugger be. Harry – drinks on me. We'll have to be sharpish, it's half seven already.

Drinks are distributed. **James** *kisses* **Jo***. Then raises his glass.*

To Benji . . .

He realises he is missing.

Where is he?

Kitty   I thought he was with you.

James   No, he went off in a huff.

Kitty   He's not been whinging already, has he?

James   He's just a bit nervous. Budge up.

James *sits next to* **Dan** *who is asleep.*

William   I'd watch yourself next to him. He pissed himself last night. Matron had to scrub him down.

Jo   Charming, that is, dropping your only pal in it.

William   It's a natural bodily function. But the last thing the lad wants for a send-off.

James   Poor sod. I hope I never get that old.

Jo   We're not even married and he wants to make uz a widow.

James   Let's sing him a lullaby.

He sings a sweet song.

> Where have all the fishees gone?
> Sleeping on the Ocean bed
> Hush now go to sleep
> Sailing on the ocean deep

Then he shouts the last line.

FISHEES IT IS MORNING!!!

Dan *wakes up with a fright.*

William   Careful. He'll piss himself again.

Jo   Bill!

Dan   Stuff the lot of yous. You'll not be laughing at my age.

Kitty   This is supposed to be a civilised send-off.

Dan *goes back to sleep.*

Jo   Oh, calm down, Kitty.

Sarah *finishes her third pint.*

Sarah   Well, I'm away then.

Jo   For Christsake, sit down. Here, have Dan's.

Jo *gives* **Dan***'s pint to* **Sarah***. Sarah sits next to* **William***. They all have to move along the bench.* **William** *complains.*

William   Hey, steady on, I'm nearly ont' floor here.

Sarah   Anyway, to the lads! And the *Hope*.

General toasting. Suddenly, **Simon** *stands up, takes a drink of his bottle.*

Simon   The *Hope*. The *Hope*. The ribs. James, Michael, where's Benji? Wait there, I have to find him.

He leaves looking for **Ben***.*

Everybody laughs. **James** *raises his glass in a mock toast.*

James   To Harry's gin and all who sail in her.

Kitty   Where the hell is he?

Michael   He'll be saying his bye-byes to his favourite photographer.

Jo   Benji!? She wouldn't touch him with a tripod.

Michael   Come on then Molly, give us a dance then.

Molly *demurs but the crowd egg her on. The band start up and the Clog dance is done. The women sing:*

> I went down to dig some tatters
> Dig some tatters for me tea
> I tripped up and dropped me bucket
> A Deckie lad come kissing me
>
> My Mother says I shouldn't marry a Deckie
> If I do he'll break my heart
> I don't care what me mother tells me
> I'll have a Deckie for my sweetheart.

Scarbro lads earn gold and silver
Whitby lads earn nowt but brass
Filey lads are not so choosy
They'll go a-courtin' an owner's lass

Tell me skipper is it right
Come tell me skipper is it true
You're not going out tonight
No bugger wants to sail with you.

The dance ends to uproarious applause.

Kitty   Where the hell's he got to?

Michael   He'll be down shortly. Drink, anyone?

William   I'm all right, son.

Sarah   Pint of same, please, Michael.

Michael   He's not going to miss his own party.

Michael *passes the drinks out.*

Kitty   You've got me worried sick now.

Jo   Calm down. He's got half an hour.

Kitty   He'll be the death of me. I've taken an advance,
you know. How'd you think I paid for this?

James   What you worried about? He's signed up, hasn't
he. Howay, Michael, give us a song.

Jed
Bound together through the land
Keep the spirit keep the way
Brothers sisters make a stand
Unity will win the day.

Jo *and* **Kitty** *boo* **Michael**'s *song.* **Sarah** *laughs at its sentiment.*

Michael   You won't be laughing come the revolution.

Jo   Revolution, my arse.

James   Ah, you load of old reactionary bastards. Keep going.

(*Sings.*)
> Bound together through the land
> Keep the spirit keep the way
> Brothers sisters make a stand
> Unity will win the day.
>
> Raise your banners high
> Strength to strength and line by line
> Unity must never die
> Raise your banner high.

James *sings the song with real passion. As he is singing we see* **Makepeace** *come along the quay. He stops and slowly comes up the corridor to watch* **James** *singing. The others are so engrossed in his song, no one notices* **Makepeace** *is there. Suddenly,* **Jed** *sees* **Makepeace** *looking on and stops. Everybody looks at* **Makepeace**.

Makepeace   Get yourself on board. You'll miss the tide!

Makepeace *turns and leaves.*

Kitty   Oh my God. Now you've done it.

Jo   What's the matter with him?

Michael   Where the hell did he come from?

Sarah   You idiot. Fancy squealing like a stuck pig when his nibs is just up the street.

Mary   He was none too chuffed, was he?

William   You'll not be singing at his table, that's for sure.

Kitty   Why on earth do you have to sing such upsetting songs?

James   For Christsake, it's my party. He's lucky I didn't plant him one. 'Get yourself on board'! Who does he think he is?

Kitty   You're just asking for trouble.

James   Oh, I'm banned from singing in me own pub, am I? Nobody tells me what to do.

Sarah   Fair's fair. If you were Makepeace you'd not want your lads preaching revolution.

James   Oh, shut up, Sarah.

Kitty   He knows how dependent I am.

James   Dependent! What are you on about. You skivvy for the fella. He's t' one dependent on you.

Jo   Give it a rest, James!

Kitty   Don't you realise – I'm going to get a right dressing down on Saturday.

James   A dressing down! Me dad and two brothers drowned so he could afford to get his house skivvied. If you weren't so bloody servile it'd be you doing t' dressing down.

Kitty   You've no idea what he's done for us.

James   He's kept your nose to the grindstone's what he's done.

Jed *reprises the first anthem.*

James
  Though the struggle brings you pain
  Though the struggle brings you tears
  Yours will be the final gain
  You shall hear the victory cheers.

Kitty   Stop it, James, Please.

James (*shouting*)   You shall hear the victory cheers.

Jo   Stop it! For God's sake, stop it!

Jo *slaps* **James** *across the face.*

The music stops dead. Everyone is silent. **James** *is furious but chastened.*

Tense silence.

Michael   Better be getting off, then.

Sarah   My goodness, is that the time!

She finishes her last pint.

Sarah, **Simon**, **Mary** and **Michael** *go off embarrassed.* **Jed** *realises the party's over. He puts a load of food in* **Trudger**'s *bag and leaves, leading* **Trudger** *out.* **Kitty** *is left mortified.* **James** *stares at* **Jo**. **Jo** *stands defiant.* **Kitty** *is almost in tears.* **Makepeace** *appears from the pub.*

Makepeace   Decided to stay, have you?

James   Talking to me?

Makepeace   Aye, I'm talking to you. You work for me now. So let's be having you.

James   I'm coming, calm yerself down.

Makepeace   Harbour police have been informed.

James   I couldn't care if you've informed the Queen. I'm just saying bye to me mam.

Kitty   It's true, sir, he's . . .

Makepeace   Where the hell's that other dunce of yours.

Kitty   We don't . . .

James   He'll be along with me.

Makepeace   I warned you once. Get going.

James   I'm not on your boat yet. I'm saying my goodbyes.

Makepeace *calmly walks across.*

Makepeace   If I were you I'd watch my tone, mister.

James   No, you watch my tone . . . Bugger off!

Makepeace *is still cool as a cucumber.*

Kitty   James. Please, don't take offence, sir – he's angry with his brother . . .

Makepeace *breaks into a smile – perhaps recognising* **James**'s *hot head.*

Makepeace   Well, there's gratitude for you. You do folk a favour and they throw it in your face. Have it your way, son, but if you're not ont' ship in five minutes I'll have the whole constabulary out to fetch you.

James   Have me fetched, will you? Who do you think I am?

Jo   James.

Makepeace   Are there any more little favours you'd like to ask, Kitty?

James   Oh, I'm a little favour, am I? Listen. You pay wages – I give my labour – I'm nobody's favour.

Makepeace   If it wasn't for your mother, I wouldn't give you time of day.

James   If it wasn't for me mam I'd knock you flat on your back. Now get to fuck.

Kitty   James, James!

A long silence.

Makepeace   Quite a party this has turned out to be. Good evening.

He turns and walks out to the quay. **Kitty** *follows him to the street, now lit by gas lamps.*

Kitty   Please, sir . . . Christopher.

Makepeace   I hope you know what you're doing, Kitty. I paid that advance in good faith.

Kitty   I know, sir.

Makepeace   Have I ever treated you badly?

Kitty   Never.

James *has followed them out. He pulls* **Kitty** *away to stop her begging.*

James   For God's sake.

Makepeace *looks at* **Kitty**.

Makepeace   I'm very sorry, Kitty.

Makepeace *walks away.* **James** *goes after him. He grabs him and swings him round.*

James   Who the fuck do you think you are?

Kitty   James.

James (*shouting back to* **Kitty**)   Get inside.

Makepeace   Any reasonable bloke about to get wed would be crawling up my arse. You've got a ten-year ban, son. I'm warning you now, you're trying my patience. Look at my grey hair, son. Think about your father.

James   The 'deep six', my dad is.

Makepeace   And mine too. Do you think you've got the monopoly on pain? Do you think you were the only fella born with a chip on his shoulder? Listen, your mother used to watch me as a bairn waiting by the bins – biting the heads off bait I was that hungry.

James   Oh, me poor heart bleeds. You weren't waiting by the bait bins when I came looking for news of me dad. You were sat in a nice warm office, counting your piles of money when I came in from t' cold.

Makepeace   Don't start, son. I'm trying to help you. I've been out in winds that would cut your ears off. I've seen things that'd have you blubbering on the floor. I got where I am by hard graft. I've been out more times than you've had cold suppers. You're young, strong, full of fire, so *use* it. Make something of yourself.

James   So I can be like you and sell every fucker else
down the river . . .

Makepeace   What century are you from, son? Listen, I'm
saying this as a friend. You have a mother. You have a mind
to get married. All right, you might have done six months –
I'm not making a song and dance about that – you might
have barked at me in a unseemly manner – but as I say,
you're young and stupid. So, I'll tell you this once only.
Treat me fair and I'll look after you – play silly buggers on t'
Hope, I'll throw the fucking book at you. Understood?

James *and* **Makepeace** *are face-to-face on the quayside.*

James   That's right, you go off to your fucking office with
your big safe and your tot of rum.

Makepeace   And my troubles, son. Do you think fleets
run themselves? I've got a hundred men to worry about.
Who do you think feeds you?

Jo *comes along the alley and watches from a distance.*

James   The fellas who tek fish out of sea. Fellas who risk
life and limb every second they're out. Who don't change
clothes for six weeks in a row? Whose hands are raw with
salt? Who have no water to wash themselves clean? Who
sleeps caged like beasts? Who leaves his wife and mother to
go begging for alms? Twelve of us go out tonight. What will
we get for our labour? What will you get? For rubbing your
hands raw while you fester by the fire.

Makepeace   For taking the risks. Who coughs up if you
lose a net or if there's a poor catch or if lightning strikes the
mast or you run the ship aground or God knows what else? I
make my money because I look after the lot. I don't see you
dipping in your pocket when there's storm damage. Yet you
go home with a full packet. I'm not a bad man, I'm not a
greedy man, I am a businessman. I'm not after the shirt off
your back. Everybody gets their due. If I do well – you do
well. If you do well – I do well. That's how it works. That's
how it *should* work. There isn't us and them. My business is

making sure you can do yours. It's not a fucking fight. We're all in this together. This isn't the nineteenth century any more. Wake up, lad. I didn't just wax my moustache and tie someone tot' railway. But there are people's livelihoods at stake here and if you make an agreement you have to bide by it. So if I were you I'd spend less time shouting at folks trying to help you, and more time looking for your brother.

Kitty   I can't . . .

Makepeace   It's past eight already. If you two aren't there in five minutes, I'll invoke article sixteen, and that's a five-quid fine before you'll've left port.

James   Go on then, fucking fine me.

Makepeace *looks at him, does not rise to the bait, turns and walks off towards the dock.* **Kitty** *chases after him.*

Kitty   Please, please, forgive him, sir.

Makepeace   I've never been spoken to like that in my life.

Kitty   He doesn't know what he's saying.

Makepeace   And you can forget coming on Saturday. We have no other use for you.

Kitty   But, sir, it's nowt to do wi' me.

Makepeace   You brought them up.

Makepeace *walks off.* **Kitty** *shouts after him.*

Kitty   Christopher!

James *is watching from under the light outside the pub.* **Kitty** *slowly walks up to him with dignity and starts to lash out at* **James**. *She thumps at him, more out of frustration and humiliation than anger. He takes the blows, then grabs her. She is crying. She continues to lash out. He hugs her, until she calms down. She is sobbing.*

Kitty   What a send-off this's turned into.

Jo *comes up to* **James** *and takes* **Kitty**, *pushing* **James** *away.*

Jo   It's all right, Kitty. James was right what he said.

Kitty   Right? What's use in being right?

Kitty *pulls herself together and pushes* **Jo** *away.*

James   You're not going after him.

Kitty   I'm going to look for Ben. They'll have him in jail.

Kitty *heads back to the pub.*

James   Aren't you going t' say goodbye?

Kitty   I'll come t' harbour.

Kitty *goes back along the alley into the pub courtyard to collect her things.* **Jo** *and* **James** *stand under the gaslight. There is an awkward pause between them.*

James   Best be off.

Jo   Be careful, won't you?

They kiss.

I'll come down with you.

James *and* **Jo** *disappear into the darkness.* **Kitty** *puts on her hat in the pub courtyard, and walks down the alley towards the quay. Suddenly, the cellar shutter opens, and a figure peeps out. It is* **Ben***. He drops the shutter which makes a noise.* **Kitty** *turns to look and sees* **Ben** *emerging from the cellar.* **Ben** *sees that* **Kitty** *is about to shout at him. He tries to keep her silent.*

Ben   Shhhh.

Kitty *storms into the courtyard.*

Kitty   You stupid little . . .

Ben   Shhh.

Kitty *clouts him around the head.*

Kitty   Don't bloody well shush me. I'll scream the place down if you don't get after your James this minute.

Ben   M- M- Mam, go. Catch him. Stop him, M- M-
Mam. S- s- stop him.

Kitty   What's the matter with you?

Ben   *Hope*'s rotten, Mam – the r- ribs are rotten. Whole
bulkhead's rotten.

Kitty   Get on that boat. Now!

Ben   P- please, Mam.

Kitty   I'll take your face off . . .

Ben   H- hit uz, h- hit uz. I don't care. Stop James. Simon
says . . .

Kitty   That pisshead.

Kitty *grabs him by the ear and is pulling him towards the quay.*

Ben   N- no. I won't. Even if you thrash me.

Kitty   It's just been int' dock.

Ben   It w- were past saving.

Kitty   I'm warning you.

Ben   I can't. You'll have to kill me. It's full o' water, Mam.

Kitty   It's bilge, you stupid idiot. Every boat's got that.

Ben *wrests himself away from his mother and runs back into the
courtyard.* **Kitty** *follows him.*

Ben   P- please, Mam, please don't make me go!

Kitty   Michael's going. Your own bloody brother's going.
I've taken money. They'll drag you through the streets.

On the quay two **Coppers**, *looking for* **Ben**, *almost stop by the
pub, but carry on towards the dock.*

Ben   I'll r- run away.

Kitty   You're not running anywhere.

Ben *tries to get past, but* **Kitty**'s *too fast for him.*

Ben   Let uz past. I w- warning you . . .

Kitty   Oh, you're brave enough now you're faced with a sixty-one-year-old woman.

Ben *collapses on to the floor.*

Ben (*shouts*)   No, no, no. You'll never see me again.

The two **Coppers** *are now far along the quay. They hear* **Ben***'s shout. They turn.*

Kitty   Get up.

She helps him to his feet. He is shaking. **Kitty** *pulls the earrings out of her pocket.*

Look, I brought you these. They were your father's.

She puts the earrings into his ears. **Ben** *is still, like a child, as she puts them in his ears. She steps back to proudly admire them. But he is weeping.*

Ben   Hide me, Mam. I'm going to drown.

Kitty   It's all right, lover. You'll get used to it.

Two **Coppers** *arrive.*

First Copper   Come on, let's be having you.

Ben *tries to make a run for it, he tries to get down the cellar, but the* **Coppers** *grab him.*

Ben   I'm not going. I'm not going. The ship's rotten.

Second Copper   Should have thought about that before you signed up then.

Ben   G- get off, get off.

They struggle with him.

Second Copper   Don't make us put cuffs on, lad.

Ben   Mam. Help me. H- help m- me.

The **Coppers** *drag* **Ben** *away but he hangs on to a wooden pillar for dear life.*

First Copper   Let go of the post.

Ben   You'll have to cut me hands off.

Kitty   Stop! Please! The lad's scared to death.

First Copper   Let go.

Both men struggle to loosen **Ben**'s *grip but can't budge him.*

Kitty   Come on, son.

To wrench **Ben** *away* **Kitty** *is forced to join in. She wrenches* **Ben**'s *hands from the post.*

Ben   Mam.

The **Coppers** *drag* **Ben** *out.* **Kitty** *is left standing.* **Harry** *emerges from the bar.*

Harry   What the hell's going on out here?

Kitty   They had to drag Ben out. I can't go down t' docks now.

She looks bereft.

The shame of it.

Harry   Never mind. There's plenty food left.

Kitty *takes no notice.* **Harry** *helps himself to a sandwich.* **Kitty** *looks towards the quay, shaken and upset.*

Harry   You all right, love?

Kitty *takes no notice.*

Harry   Pickled onion?

Kitty *does not react.* **Harry** *shrugs, pops an onion in his mouth, collects some glasses and disappears into the pub.* **Kitty** *is left devastated. In the distance we hear the noise of a horn signalling the Good Hope's departure. Slowly the pier fills with townsfolk who watch the ship gradually disappear into the darkness.*

Act Three

Night. A storm is raging.

Kitty's *tiny house is set centre stage against a panorama of the harbour. It is dwarfed by the masts and sails of scores of vessels blowing violently in the gale that is sweeping through the town.*

The noise of the storm is tremendous, the masts jolt about perilously. Lights come up on the inside of **Kitty**'s *parlour, a frail oasis of light and warmth in the turbulent pitch of the town.*

Every time the door opens, the storm shrieks and breaks into the tiny cottage, but for now, inside, it is relatively calm, with the sound of a storm as if observed from inside.

Kitty *is asleep, covered in a blanket.* **Jo** *is reading. There is a knock at the door.* **Jo** *tiptoes to answer it. She opens it and we hear the shriek of wind outside. Enter* **Clementine** *and* **Arthur**, *the bookkeeper, carrying a tureen. The door closes.* **Kitty** *wakes with a start.*

Kitty   What is it?

Clementine   It's only us. I've never seen such weather.

Kitty *coughs and tries to get up.*

Jo   You sit down.

Clementine   How are you feeling? I've brought some soup and a few eggs. Arthur, Arthur.

Arthur   Beg your pardon?

Clementine   The eggs.

Arthur   The what?

Clementine   He's an absolute trial – deaf as a post. The EGGS.

Arthur   No need to shout.

Kitty   Has it calmed down yet?

Clementine   If anything it's getting worse. I've brought you a chicken broth, Kitty. It's delicious.

Clementine *gestures to* **Arthur** *to give* **Kitty** *the chicken broth. He puts it down.* **Clementine** *takes off the lid and looks in dismay.*

Clementine   For crying out loud, there's hardly any left.

Arthur   You try keeping pan o' soup steady int' force-nine gale.

Clementine   When we set out there was half a chicken in here.

Arthur   Beg your pardon, Miss, can't hear a thing with t' wind.

Kitty   Thank you, Miss.

Arthur *puts the eggs on the table too.*

Clementine   Arthur, there are only four eggs here.

Arthur   That's all you gave me.

Arthur *is setting up the food, much to* **Clementine***'s consternation.*

Clementine   Get out of the way.

Clementine *pushes* **Arthur** *out of the way, as she does so, we hear a crack. They all look.*

Arthur   Oh buggery.

Arthur *puts his hand in his pocket and retrieves his keys dripping with yolk. He accidentally brings out a chicken drumstick, also covered with yolk.*

Clementine   You thieving scoundrel. Taking food from a sick woman.

Arthur   But there were too much for one.

Arthur *seems more perturbed about the mess than being told off.*

Jo   I expect you fancied a nice chicken omelette, when you got home.

Arthur   You'd never've known if you hadn't pushed me.

Clementine   I'll make sure Daddy knows about this. Now get lost.

Arthur   You're not sending me back out right away.

Kitty   Let him stay. It's no crime being hungry.

Clementine   It serves him right.

Arthur   But I might slip.

Clementine   You'll just have to be careful.

Arthur looks put upon and reluctantly leaves. Again, the gale howls through the house as the door is opened.

Clementine   You have to count your fingers every time he shakes your hand. How is the soup?

Kitty   Delicious, Miss, I don't know how to thank you. Does your father know you're here?

Clementine   No. And I think it's best he doesn't. He's still apoplectic over James. He'll get over it. Come on, Jo, come look at the sea with me. It's astounding.

Jo   That all right, Kitty?

Kitty   You can't go t' beach in this.

There is a huge cracking sound.

Jo   What the hell was that?

*Enter **William**.*

William   Bloody hell.

Jo   William!?

William   Nearly killed me.

Kitty   What was it?

William   Tree, smashed right down on next door. Near took my neck off.

Kitty   I hope they're not in.

Jo   What the hell are you doing running around in this?

William   Fetching doctor. Dan's sick.

Clementine   What's the matter?

Jo   Sit down, will you.

Jo gives him a cup of tea.

William   Can't keep owt down – brought up bacon and beans all over t' show.

Clementine   What on earth are you feeding him bacon and beans for!?

William   Unfortunately, Matron had run out of caviar. He's talking weird – stuff about putting out lines – I'm scared, Kitty. I told her to get doctor this morning, but she wouldn't listen. I've told Simon to get cart and take uz down.

Jo   Simon?

William   He's on his way.

Clementine   You'll end up off a cliff with him driving.

William   No, no, he's sober.

Jo   And I'm a Dutchman. You might be daft enough to get on his cart but doctor'll think twice.

There is a howling and cracking from outside.

William   Christ . . . listen to it. He's in a bad way. He's terrified he won't pull through.

Clementine   Who wouldn't be?

William   I dunno. If it were my turn tomorrow, I'd say: *so be it.* We all have to go some time. Don't see what there is to

be scared on. Death's not a 'thing', it's not summat out
there you can fight or flee from; it can't rip you apart or tear
your heart out. It's life does that. Death's not a 'thing' you
can touch or feel or hear or take a look at. Death's nothing.
Nothing. You don't get scared 'bout before you was born.
What's there to fear of t' other end? . . . don't laugh . . . God
takes us, we take the fishes. That's the order. There's
nothing more to know. Nothing to be feared on. Many's the
time, I've been on deck gutting herring, there's few as fast as
I, and you push the knife in and you look int' eye of that
creature, an eye full of fear and . . . intelligence . . .
flickering, asking, am I less blessed than thee? And I think,
maybe in ten year, maybe in fifty, not one of us out there
will still be here. Say in ninety year not one of us on t' entire
globe, that's now living, will be here. No, we are all as
blessed as each other. We take the fishes, God takes us. One
barrel tips int' other. There's no chance about it. That's the
order, there's none escape – men nor fishes. Tis only time
that separates us one from other. Sooner or later we will all
be one. Returned to nothing, from whence we came. That's
the facts, lass. Nay, you're not scared of death – death is
nowt, so there is nought to be scared on. No, lass, it's *life*
you're scared on.

Pause.

Kitty   Have you been drinking?

William   I'm lucky to get cuppa tea round here.

Kitty   I'm worried about next door. Best see they're all
right.

Jo   Sit down, will you. I'll go.

Kitty   No, no. I'm feeling better.

She's up and off.

Jo   You stubborn old cow. Yous stay here.

Kitty *leaves.* **Jo** *follows. The wind howls through.*

William　Careful of the lamp.

Clementine　I'll thank the Lord when the *Hope*'s back.

William　No ship'll be safe tonight. Least *Hope*'s old – old ships are last to go down.

Clementine　You think so?

William　Tis known fact, Miss.

He takes the opportunity to pour himself a dram.

Will you take a drop?

Clementine　No, no. (*Pause.*) But I'll pray for the *Hope* tonight.

William　Good luck to you, but the *Jacob*'s out, and t' *Expectation* . . . you'll be praying for a lot of ships, love.

Clementine　But the *Hope*'s rotten . . .

Clementine *stops dead.* **William** *looks at her.*

William　Who said that?

Clementine　No one. I mean . . . it was in dock, wasn't it.

William　Who said it's rotten?

Clementine　No one. I was letting my imagination get the better of me.

Jo *and* **Kitty** *come back.*

Clementine　Anyway, let's stop dwelling on all this. How was it, Kitty?

Kitty　Went straight through their window. They must be down at their Tony's.

Jo　Lucky they were out.

Kitty　What a night. My poor boys . . . Benji will be terrified . . . so nearly home.

Jo　Here, get warm, Kitty. Will you have a cup, Miss?

Enter **Simon** *and* **Mary**.

Simon   What a blasted gale.

Mary *comes in. She is very distressed, crying.*

Kitty   Are you all right, pet?

Mary   I'm thinking of Michael.

Kitty   Come on, sweetheart. Look at Jo . . . her man's a seaman too . . . seamen's wives don't cry . . . silly lass . . . give her a cup of something.

Mary   But it's the sixth week . . .

William   Stop wailing 'fore you've been hit, lass. Is the coach ready, driver?

Simon   I'm not doing this for fun, you know . . . if it wasn't for Dan . . .

Jo   It'll do you good, Simon.

Simon   Listen, it were a night like this I lost Katherine. She were pregnant and I were taking her down t' road to doctor. The wind were howling and we hit t' rock and whole thing came off road. She were lying there. There were nowt I could do. By t' time I got doctor she were gone. Just lying there by the road. Anyway. We best go, Billy.

Kitty   Go easy, Simon.

Simon   Don't worry.

William   Night, all.

Kitty   Take care.

William *and* **Simon** *wrap up and leave. The relentless wind howls through the cottage. A long silence.*

Mary   Last night. I thought I saw Michael. I don't know if I was awake or asleep. I was just lying and there was a knock – at the window – and I sat bolt upright – and I looked about but there was nothing – then it came again (*She* *knocks.*) – so I got up and slowly went to the window – and looked – nothing – there was nothing there. Then just as I was going to lie down – knock – and I spun round and there was Michael's face – at the window – pale as milk – then there was nothing – just darkness . . .

Kitty *is spooked.*

Kitty   Three knocks?

Mary   That's right.

Jo   Oh for Christsake. The pair of you.

There is a sudden knocking. They all jump.

Enter **Susan** *and* **Sarah**. *Another gust bursts through. The old women struggle to shut the door against the massive gale.*

Susan   It's only us.

Sarah   You look like you've seen a ghost.

Jo   Thank the Lord you've arrived. It's like a morgue in here.

Sarah   What a night. I've got sand blowing down my bloomers.

Susan   I couldn't stand it at home with no one to talk to. Two mooring posts gave way . . .

Kitty   Two mooring posts?

Sarah   It's a terrible night. And you two with sons out.

Susan   Aye, young Toby's a good un – barely twelve – you should have seen him two months ago – when the *Anna* brought back Stephen – what a comfort he was to me – a proper little man – we stayed up right through the night talking – I swear that laddie's wiser than I am.

Sarah   Did you know if you wear red spectacles you don't get seasick.

Jo   Here we go.

Sarah   It's a known fact.

Jo   Oh aye, like you've tried.

Sarah   Listen, I've been out plenty.

Jo   When?

Sarah   When my Ian were alive.

Clementine   You were married!?

Sarah   I know I'm no oil painting but I have my charms. (*She winks.*) Yes, I were married. And a fine head of hair he had too. Fair dos, he smashed the house up most days. But beggars can't be choosers, eh.

Jo   Tell us about the penknife, Sair.

Sarah   You don't want to hear that old yarn.

Jo   Drink anybody?

Sarah   You've twisted me arm. I bought my hubby a penknife – cost a fortune it did, leather sheaf, the lot – he goes off – comes back five week later – so I says where's penknife – it cost a fortune, that did. He says – you never bought me a effin' penknife – I says I did – it was in an effin' sheath – 'scuse my French. So I says – you've lost the effin' penknife, haven't you – he says he's never seen it in his life. Any rate, one thing leads to another, he goes mental, smashes the place up. Plates all over. I thumped him with the poker, et cetera, et cetera. So things quieten down. He takes his boots off to go to bed. Bang. He looks down. There's the effin' penknife. Been stuck in his shoe for six weeks and he never even noticed. But a fine head of hair for a Welshman.

Clementine   He kept his boots on for six weeks.

Sarah   Oh aye. Had to scrub him with soda. Covered in lice, he were.

Clementine   How disgusting.

Sarah   Any rate, temper got the better of him. He slipped on the *Expedition* trying to hit the skipper with a herring rake. Straight over the side. Never heard of again. Still don't understand why I can't remarry.

Clementine   Whoever's stopping you?

Jo   The entire male population of the British Isles.

Sarah   Thank you. Whoever makes up these effin' regulations. You've got to put three ads in t' paper – just in case he managed to swim a hundred miles to dry land and start up a new life in Bridlington. If no one comes forward, you're in the clear. Where am I going to get the money for three adverts?

Jo   Where you going to get another husband.

They all laugh except **Mary**.

Mary   Listen to the wind.

Jo   Look, put Michael out of your mind.

Mary   I'm not thinking about Michael . . . Tony, my brother.

She sobs.

Clementine   Your brother?

Jo   Can we not change the subject.

Clementine   It's all right. You can tell us.

Jo   For God's sake . . .

Mary   It was his second trip – it was a stormy night – and he were hit by the jib – suddenly he was overboard – he were t' cableman. The skipper held out a herring rake and he grabbed it. But it was too slippy – his hand slid off – and he fell back into t' sea, so bosun gets a broom and he grabbed on to that while three of them pulled him – just as he got to t' side the head came off – they threw out a line –

and that snapped 'nall – and that was it. Couldn't see him in t' dark. They went round and round for hours.

Clementine   That's terrible –

Mary   Said he knew it was coming – he sat up crying the night afore. They thought it was because of Mam, but he said no – he just felt something bad coming.

Clementine   Oh, Mary.

Mary   That's what drove me dad to drink.

No one says a word. They listen to the wind howling.

Jo   I really think we should talk about something else.

Clementine   No. You tell us something, Kit. You've been through so much, haven't you?

Kitty   These aren't just tales, sweetheart. These are people's lives. It isn't some big adventure story. Those boys out there are separated from eternity by a plank the thickness of your thumb. It's all right for some. I passed the Mayor's house last night and they were all sat down to big plates of shellfish all steaming – livers on t' side – children with their hands together. And God forgive me – I thought it were wrong – I thought it were wrong for the Mayor to be sitting there – with the wind howling – and the fish coming from the same water as t' dead – I know it's daft – but you know what I mean.

And it made me think of Jack. You see, my husband was a one in a million. Could taste the sand they brought up for depth readings and tell exactly where they were. If he said fifty-sixth latitude, sure as eggs is eggs, it were the fifty-sixth. Once, he drifted for a week with a ship full of men. Fog so thick, they couldn't see floats on the long line. Nowt to eat or drink. Finally, the hull broke up – you should have heard him tell it – he swam with with his mate George to bit of floating hull. Three more nights he hung there – said he'd never forget it. But George were too weak to hang on and started to slip, so Jack stuck his knife int' hull so's George

had summat to grip to – near cut three fingers off – and
each time George fell Jack swam out and pulled him back.
Three days int' water. And he said on t' third George went
mad – he didn't know whether it were from loss of blood or
fear – but his eyes went like cat's eyes – and he was
screaming Satan was in him – and the blood was gushing
over the bit of boat – even the waves couldn't wash it away
– and just as dawn broke George swam away – and Jack
tried to go after but George just disappeared – just like that
– Jack were picked up by a cargo vessel. He was a one in a
million, my Jack. Three years later he went out on t'
Clementine – and never came back. Not a word. Not a
hatch nor a buoy were found. My Jack and two eldest. And
every day when the kids shouted: 'There's a ball up, there's
a ball up,' I'd run down to t' quay, and the ship would come
in, and I'd walk back alone. And you do that for weeks, and
then it's been months. And every time you hope as if it was
the first time. But then one time you hear it. And you don't
go down. And you can't live with yourself for not going
down. But you can't bear living if you do. And every day
that's all you think about. Then gradually you catch yourself
thinking about something else. And soon you're used to it.
And after a few years you can't even remember their face
too well. Yes, you feel guilty, but soon you're thanking God.
For having forgot. No one should be haunted . . . Well,
that's my story. Same as every seaman's wife – it's a high
price to pay for fish, that's for sure.

Clementine   Please God – don't let any ships perish
tonight!

Jo (*screams*)   For God's sake. Shut up! Shut up! Shut up!
You're driving me mad!

Clementine   Jo – is anything the matter?

Jo   Ships go down. We all know that. We all know about
her husband, and her brother, and uncle Tom Cobley and
all – we all know your damned stories. Let me tell you a
story. My dad drowned. He drowned, he drowned, he

drowned, he drowned, he drowned. (*Screaming at*
Clementine.) What have you got to say to that? . . . Go to
hell.

*She leaves wearing only her skirt and blouse. The rain pours in for a
second before she slams the door behind her.*

Clementine   Perhaps I should go?

Kitty   No, love. She'll calm herself down – she's been
under a lot of strain.

Clementine   No, it's getting late, Kit – and to be quite
honest I don't think your niece appreciates my company –
not that I mind, but. . . is anybody going my way?

Sarah   If one goes we all go. Less chance of being blown
away.

Kitty   Please, don't.

Mary   No, Kitty. You get some sleep.

Clementine   Bye, Kitty.

Mary   Bye, Aunt Kit . . .

They all get up and go to the door.

Kitty   Thank you again, Miss, for the soup and eggs.

Clementine   Really, it's nothing.

Kitty   Bye, Miss. Bye, Mary. Bye, Sarah – if you see Jo
send her in, won't you?

*They go. She clears up the cups. The wind howls around the house. She
looks anxiously out of the window. She starts to clean the house, but
after some time is overcome with the futility of it all. She moves her
chair closer to the hearth, and sits uncomfortably, moving around trying
to be comfortable. She finally stares into the fire, with a morose torpor.
She almost subconsciously starts to mutter a rosary.*

Suddenly, the door bursts open. **Jo** *enters, she is soaked to the skin.
Exhausted, freezing and blasted by the storm – she seems physically*

shocked. **Kitty** *tries not to be alarmed by her presence.* **Jo** *shivers and starts to undress.*

Pause.

Kitty   It was good of the girl to bring eggs and chicken through that wind.

Pause.

Jo   Your sons are out in ten times worse.

Kitty   She didn't have to.

Jo   They're out for *her* father.

Kitty   And us.

Jo   It's *wild*, Kitty.

Kitty   You seen it?

Jo   Half the parade's gone . . . I hate those stories, Kit.

Kitty   Were you like this when he was in the Navy? A seaman's wife can't be weak, love. In a week or so there'll be more storms and more after that.

Jo   We shouldn't have sent Ben – I taunted him till the end.

Jo *is naked. She goes to the window and opens it letting the gale blow against her. She roars in anger into the storm. The wind causes havoc, blowing the whole contents of the house into a maelstrom. The light goes out.* **Kitty** *rushes to her and pulls her away and closes the window. She relights the lamp.* **Jo** *is on the floor.*

Kitty   What are you doing?

Jo   I don't know.

Kitty *covers her with a blanket, and helps her up to sit at the table.* **Jo** *is sobbing.* **Kitty** *sits back down allowing her space.*

Pause.

Jo   Kitty. I'm . . .

Kitty   I know. You should have told me, he's my son. Let us pray.

Jo   I don't want to pray.

Kitty   You have to, child.

Jo   What will be will be.

Kitty   Listen. Nothing's going to happen.

Jo *bangs her head on the table, repeatedly. Slowly at first then really smashing her head.* **Kitty** *watches her till she stops.* **Jo** *is crying.*

Jo   The wind.

Kitty *sits, opens a bible . . .*

Kitty

They that go down to the sea in ships,
   that do business in great waters;

Those see the work of the LORD,
   and his wonders in the deep.

For he commandeth and raiseth the stormy wind
   which lifteth up the waves thereof.

They mount up to the heaven, they go down again to the depths;
   their soul is melted because of trouble.

They reel to and fro, and stagger like a drunken man
   and are at their wits' end.

Then they cry unto the LORD in their trouble,
   and he bringeth them out of their distress.

As **Kitty** *reads, the wind blows stronger round the house. The storm whips up and rips through the town. We hear glass breaking. The sails are battered by the wind and the chaos overwhelms the little house, which seems to recede into the distance as the storm engulfs the stage. The high-pitched whining of the storm turns into an eerie small air on the pipes. The light goes out. Blackness, calm.*

Act Four

Morning. Winter.

*Whitby Town Square. The cobbled street is covered in snow. In the foreground is **Makepeace**'s office, cut away so we can see inside. It is raised up with windows that survey the whole dockside. It is reached by a wooden staircase that goes down to the quay. Through the windows, and to the rear we see the dockside, endless rows of masts, all covered in snow.*

Snow is falling. The small air merges into The Whitby Carol. In the distance we see a huddle of carol singers, we hear them singing.

Hark, Hark what news the angels bring
Glad tidings of a newborn king
Born of a maid, a virgin pure
Born without sin, from guilt secure.

Behold he comes and leaves the skies
Awake ye slumbering, mortals rise
Awake to joy and hail the morn
A saviour of this world was born.

*Inside **Makepeace**'s office a fire is blazing. There is a rail behind which a bench forms a sort of waiting room by the door. **Arthur** is putting up Christmas decorations. When he is done he looks out of the window and, seeing the coast is clear, he sneaks over to the cigar box on **Makepeace**'s desk and takes a couple, pushing them in his pocket, then takes a whisky bottle from behind some books on **Makepeace**'s bookshelf. He has a nip, then another, then sees that it is evident someone has been drinking so fills it to the right level with some water and secretly puts it back.*

*We hear someone trudging through the snow. We see it is **Simon**. He walks to the office, comes up the steps and through the door.*

Simon   Where's Makepeace?

Arthur   Born in a barn?

Simon *shuts the door and comes into the room.*

Arthur   Behind that gate, thank you.

Simon   Where is he?

Arthur   Out.

Simon   Well, tell me. What's news?

Arthur   What's what news?

Simon   The *Hope*.

Arthur   For Christsake, not that malarkey. As soon as we hear . . .

Simon   So . . . nothing.

Arthur   Nothing.

Simon   It's nine weeks tomorrow.

Arthur   The *Jacob* came back with 190 barrels after fifty-nine days . . .

Simon   You know something.

Arthur   Don't be daft, Simon.

Simon   You know something.

Arthur   You been boozing?

Simon   Not a drop.

Arthur   Well, it's high time you did. What do you mean I know something? Do you think I keep fleet on t' end of string? Look, they've been gone eight weeks. His nibs is sick to death wi' worry. What do you want me to do about it?

Simon   I told you when it was int' dock.

Arthur   You told me a load of drunken horseshit so's you could get yourself the price of a drink.

Simon   You were there – with him and his daughter. It were plain as day. It were rotten. You saw with your own eyes.

Arthur   You could barely stand up. Do you really expect us to take you serious.

Simon   Bastard.

Simon *goes for him.*

Arthur   Get behind that gate. Even if you weren't 'pallatic'. You're not even a qualified shipwright. Are you seriously telling me cos you had a shufty down below afore knocking off t' Sailor's we should've had her int' scrapyard? Look. A certificate of seaworthiness. Know where that come from? The insurers. The insurers, Simon.

Simon   It's got nowt to do with it. I don't care who's been paid off. If they don't come back it's *murder*. There's blood ont' all your hands.

Arthur   If I were you, I'd have meself a jar before you get in trouble. It's Christmas.

Mary *comes in.*

Simon   I thought I told you to stay home. There's nowt.

Mary   No news then?

Simon   Just murder. (*To* **Arthur**.) You hear me.

Mary *and* **Simon** *leave.* **Arthur** *sneaks another nip of whisky.* **Sarah** *comes along the quay.*

The telephone rings. **Arthur** *jumps with fright. It rings and rings.* **Arthur** *looks at it nervously. Finally, he plucks up the courage to answer it.*

Arthur   Hello. Hello. Sorry, can you speak up? What? No. No. This is Arthur Sedgwick speaking. Sorry, can you speak up? No, this is his bookkeeper. I'm afraid he is currently incommoded . . . No, no . . . Sorry, can you please call back, please? That's right, ten minutes. Yes. Thank you.

As **Arthur** *is on the phone,* **Sarah** *comes in.* **Arthur** *finishes the call and slams the earpiece down with relief. He is clearly terrified of the phone.*

Sarah   Morning, handsome.

Arthur   What do *you* want?

Sarah   Me hands are cold. I thought you could warm them up.

Arthur   Stay behind that gate.

Sarah   Oh, a proper tease. Don't fret, lover, I won't take no for an answer.

Arthur   I'm warning you. Stay behind that gate. Or there'll be trouble.

Sarah   No news, I take it.

Arthur   No. There's nothing, funnily enough.

Sarah   No need to jump down me throat. Seven families, lucky most were single lads.

Arthur   Can we get to t' point?

Just as **Sarah** *is launching into her speech.* **William** *comes running along the dock. He is in very bad shape. He slips and hurts himself on the icy cobbles, but gets up and makes great haste towards the office.*

Sarah   Well, as you no doubt know I am currently engaged in a relationship with a certain bargemaster from Saltburn who is currently here with a cargo of manure. However, on account of my husband being deemed neither alive nor dead I am unable to make an honest woman of myself.

Arthur   What's this got to do with *me*?

Sarah   I need an official statement.

Arthur   Look, I can't help you. All you have to do is put three notices in t' paper . . .

William *is rushing up the stairs.*

Sarah   How'm I supposed to do that? I can't even get a widow's pension.

Arthur   Look, it's not my fault. You need to go into town and . . .

Enter **William**, *worn and exhausted. He speaks with great urgency.*

William   What news of the *Hope*? What news of the boys?

Arthur   There is no news.

William   No, there's news . . . You must have heard.

Arthur   There isn't any news. It doesn't matter how many times a day you come in here. There. Is. Nothing. To tell you.

William   No. We've heard . . . The Commissioner . . . a telegram. Please, Arthur . . . We're demented . . .

Arthur   Really, Bill . . . there's nothing.

William   M' niece is home – cleaning up for t' priest . . . I know there's news . . . even if you won't . . .

Arthur   Who's been filling your head with this rubbish?

William   Commissioner's clerk . . . saw telegram be delivered.

William *looks at* **Arthur**.

Arthur   I'm sorry, William.

William *realises* **Arthur** *is telling the truth. He looks at* **Sarah** *and* **Arthur**. *He is lost and broken. He turns and leaves in silence.*

Sarah   What d'ya think?

Arthur   Anything's possible.

Sarah   What does Makepeace reckon 'bout *Hope*?

Outside, **William** *passes* **Clementine** *without acknowledgement.*

Arthur   What's anyone reckon? Nine weeks. After that storm. Rations for a month. If they'd landed abroad we'd've heard. No. Not a snowball's chance in hell.

Enter **Clementine**, *carrying her camera.*

Clementine   Was that William just in here? I almost didn't recognise him. He's aged twenty years.

Sarah   Took it bad when Dan died . . . he's no one to argue with no more.

Clementine   Oh, it's freezing. But the view over the harbour is quite breathtaking.

She warms her hands on the fire as she takes her coat off.

The phone rings. No one answers it. **Clementine** *looks up at* **Arthur**.

Arthur   It'll be for your dad. They called a while ago.

It rings.

Clementine   Well, aren't you going to answer it?

Arthur   Couldn't you get it, Miss?

Clementine   Oh, for goodness sake.

She answers it.

Hello. Yes. No . . . Yes. I'm afraid he's not here. No, this is his daughter.

Arthur   He'll just be a few minutes.

Clementine *tries to shush him up.*

Clementine   Sorry, what did you say? You'll have to speak up . . . sorry, a hatch . . .

She screams and drops the phone.

Arthur   What's wrong, Miss?

Clementine   I can't listen.

Arthur   What is it, Miss? The Commissioner?

Clementine   Ben has been washed up. It's over.

Sarah   Ben? Ben?

Clementine   A telegram from Berwick. Just a hatch and a body.

Makepeace *comes through the door.*

Makepeace   What is it?

Arthur   The *Hope*.

Makepeace *blanches.*

Arthur   Commissioner's on the line.

Makepeace   The Shipping Commissioner?! (*To* **Sarah**.) What on earth is she doing here? Get out.

Sarah   I . . . I . . .

Makepeace *is mortified.*

Makepeace   Get out, woman.

Sarah *leaves.* **Makepeace** *picks up the phone, clearly shaken.*

Makepeace   Hello? Who is this? Yes, it's me. A telegram . . . from . . . I see . . . You'll have to speak up . . . Oh, this is a blow . . . this is a real blow . . . how did they recognise him? . . . Earrings? . . . skipper of the *Expectation* . . . What was the *Expectation* doing up there? . . . I see . . . no, no . . . This is an awful business . . . so we don't need to send someone . . . no . . . thank you . . . thank you . . . this is awful for us all . . . yes, I'd appreciate the official report as soon as . . . God bless you.

He hangs up the receiver.

Twelve men. This is a real blow.

Arthur   It's a miracle young Ben was washed up at all. With the *Clementine* . . .

Makepeace   Yes, yes. We know!

He is visibly shaken. He takes his secret bottle and pours a drink to calm his nerves.

What were you thinking of taking the call with that woman around.

Arthur   We didn't know.

Makepeace   Half the town'll be here in five minutes. This is a real blow.

Clementine   This is your fault. Why didn't you listen?

Makepeace   Listen?

Clementine   To Simon. The shipwright.

Makepeace   He's a drunk.

Clementine   He wasn't drunk when he warned us.

Makepeace   He couldn't stand up straight.

Clementine   I was there, God save me, I'm guilty too.

Makepeace   Guilty? Guilty! What sort of language is that? It was an accident.

Clementine   You heard him. He said it was a floating coffin. You said in any event it would be the last trip for the *Hope*.

Makepeace   This is nothing to do with you.

Clementine   It's to do with all of us. There's blood on all our hands.

Makepeace   Oh, that damned boarding school. That damned expensive liberal claptrap. You can hang around the quay and fraternise with every drunken beggar you see but don't stick your nose in matters that you don't understand. He was no shipwright. The only thing he's expert at is the drinking of gin. A floating coffin? For crying out loud – the *Victory*, the *King Billy*, the *Expedition*, the *Explorer* – I could go on all day – the entire fishing fleet of the North Sea are 'floating coffins'. The whole merchant navy's a floating coffin. The trouble with you pampered philanthropists is none of you want to deal with hard fact.

Why do you think the underwriters inspect ships once a
year? Do you think when I ring up the insurer and ask for
seven thousand pounds he's going to write me a cheque for
an unseaworthy vessel? You don't understand what you're
saying.

Clementine   Well, if I was shipowner . . .

Makepeace   Oh, God help the shipping industry when
we get owners crying over scuffed knuckles and taking
portraits of the crew every time they set sail. Look, I am a
father at the head of a hundred families. I am responsible
for the livelihoods of most of this town. There is a system.
Look, there is a certificate. The *Hope* was seaworthy.
Seaworthy. I've been to Greenland in worse-looking vessels.
This is *business*. There's no time to be sentimental – we've
too much responsibility to get hysterical. I will not have that
language used in this office. This is a tragedy, for all of us.

Clementine *stands chastened.*

Clementine   I won't say another word.

Arthur   I've found the ship's roll. William Hest – thirty-
seven, married four children, Henry Adams – thirty-five.

Makepeace *takes the roll from* **Arthur** *and continues reading it.*

Makepeace   Married four children. Stephen Pine –
twenty-five, married one child – Geoffery Littleton – single,
twenty-six. Neil Bloom – thirty-five, married seven children.
George Wainwright, twenty-four, married no children –

As he is reading his litany **Susan** *comes into the office, followed by*
Mary. *They are confronted with* **Makepeace** *reading the roll. He
is obviously upset and they stand dumbstruck as he reads out the names.*

Solomon Berg – twenty-five, one child, Peter Jeffries –
twenty-five, two children. Michael Staines, nineteen. James
Fitzgerald – twenty-five. Benjamin Fitzgerald – nineteen.

He looks at **Susan**.

Toby Kemp – twelve.

Long devastated silence.

I'm so sorry, Mrs Kemp.

Mary   No. It can't be.

Makepeace   The Commissioner of Wrecks at Berwick telegraphed our Commissioner this morning. Benjamin Fitzgerald was washed ashore.

Susan   Oh Mary mother of Jesus . . .

Mary *bursts into hysterical laughter.* **Clementine** *goes to comfort her but* **Mary** *lashes out.*

Mary   Get off. Get off me.

Makepeace   I'm so sorry. It is God's will. We haven't had such a disaster in years. Please, I know it's no comfort but I'll pay your son's wages in full. Today, if you want it.

He realises this is no comfort. **Susan** *is bereft.*

I think it's best if you went home – this is no place to grieve. Try to rest and accept the inevitable.

Mary   I don't want to go home. I want to die.

Clementine   Cry, Mary, it will do you good. Just cry, my poor love . . .

Mary *shakes her head.*

Mary   No, no, not in front of you. I'll do that on my own.

Mary *looks* **Clementine** *in the eye, then she takes* **Susan** *and leaves.*

Arthur *looks at* **Makepeace**.

Makepeace   What's the matter with you? Are you going to sit on your arse all day? Get the Widows and Orphans' fund.

Arthur   It's locked away, sir.

Makepeace   For good reason.

Makepeace *throws him the keys.*

Arthur   Thank you, sir.

Arthur *opens a safe and takes out a large cash box.*

Makepeace   How many's on already?

Arthur   Twenty-five widows – and thirty-five children.
The fund'll never stand it. We'll have to put out an appeal.

Makepeace *crumples on his desk.*

Clementine   I'll never get over this.

Arthur   You will, Miss. There's plenty ships lost at sea. In
year or two the *Hope*'ll seem irrelevant.

He looks out to sea.

Just look at it now – smooth as a mill pond – who would
think it could take all those souls?

Jo *and* **William** *enter.* **Jo** *is extremely distraught.*

Clementine   Jo.

William   We had to get out of house.

Makepeace   Please, take this seat.

He places her by the fire.

Come by t' fire. You've heard.

Jo   Ben. But what 'bout James? Maybe . . .

Makepeace   Hush child, there's no comfort.

Jo   Maybe it isn't Benji – how can they tell?

Makepeace   His earrings. The skipper of *Expectation* . . .

Jo   What if they're wrong? Please, sir, give me some
money. I'll go up to Berwick myself, sir.

Makepeace   This is madness. Please, my sweet thing . . .

Jo   But if it is Benji, he'll need to be buried.

Makepeace   Please, it's all taken care of.

Under this conversation, **Simon** *has made a drunken progress through the streets and haphazardly comes up the stairs. He bursts in and stands swaying in the door. He is drunk, confused, with a wild look in his eye and a knife in his hand. The room stops dead at his arrival.*

Simon   I . . . I . . . heard . . .

Makepeace   Get out of here. You're drunk!

Simon   I . . . I . . . won't kill anyone . . . I don't mean you any harm . . .

Makepeace   Arthur, fetch a constable . . .

Simon   Stay there. I'll go of my own accord. I just came to say . . . I were right, weren't I? . . . I were right 'bout the *Hope*.

Makepeace   Get him out!

Simon   Don't come near me . . . (*He brandishes his knife.*) . . . I just came to say . . . to say that I were right . . . I warned you . . . admit it, I warned you when she was int' dock.

Makepeace   The man's raving.

Simon   Well, ask t' bookkeeper and daughter. They was there.

Makepeace   The man's a liar and a drunk. This is not the place, there are people grieving. Arthur, did you hear me?

Simon (*to* **Arthur**)   You were there. I showed you.

Arthur   No, I wasn't. Even if I were I wouldn't've heard owt, would I?

Makepeace   Did you hear this derelict warn us, darling?

Clementine   Father . . .

Makepeace   Come on, tell everybody. As my daughter, tell us what you heard.

Long pause.

Clementine   I can't remember.

Simon   Oh, you are so low. I told you it were rotten.
Rotten!

Makepeace   You asked my daughter and my bookkeeper
to bear witness. You heard what they said. Now be on your
way.

William   Wait . . .

Makepeace   What the dickens is it now? Did you warn
me too?

William   No, no . . . I remember . . . She knew. She
might deny it . . . But she knew. . . night of storm. At
Kit's . . .

Clementine   No, I . . .

William   Yes. Yes, you did . . . and I said: 'Miss, you're
making it up *cos if your father knew* . . . knew *Hope* were
rotten . . .

Jo   You started to cry – you were afraid the ship'd go
down – I was there – Susan was there. Oh, you nest of
vipers.

Makepeace   Vipers, is it? We who feed you year in, year
out. Have you lost your mind? Surely you believe us before
some drunken lunatic.

Jo   Believe YOU!? She's a liar but you are worse.

Makepeace   Get out.

Jo   You had Benji dragged on by police. You bastard. You
murdering bastard. No need to show us out. James was too
big a man to be pushed around. If I stayed here I would spit
in your face, sir.

Makepeace   For Kitty's sake I'll assume the news got the
better of you. The *Hope* was completely seaworthy.

'Seaworthy' – do you hear? Have I not lost too? Have you any idea what this'll cost me? And what if the drunk *had* warned me? What responsible businessman is expected to take decisions on the whims of an inebriate who can't get work anywhere up the coast cos he's too pissed to handle a mallet?

Simon   I told you . . . It was a floating coffin . . . It was the truth.

Makepeace   It was an accident. There was a storm.

Jo   Just give me some money. I'll go to Berwick – please, I won't say anything more.

Makepeace   You'll not have a penny. Not after what you've said, young lady.

Jo   I didn't know what I was saying – I don't – I don't know anything.

Makepeace (*softly, with great compassion*)   Please. Go home.

Simon   You're worse than the devil.

Simon *leaves, the others follow.*

Makepeace (*to* **Clementine**)   And you. Never set foot in this office again.

Clementine   How could I? . . . How could I ever respect you . . . or myself?

She leaves.

Makepeace   This is insanity.

Outside we hear **Trudger**'*s one-man band singing a carol.*

Makepeace   Oh, for Christsake . . .

He goes to the window.

Get lost, will you.

He sits down exhausted. He drinks some whisky and starts to read the roll of dead men.

Makepeace   'William Hest – thirty-seven . . .'

Tears well up in his eyes. He can no longer continue. He crumples the paper up and throws it away. He grabs the bottle and throws that across the room. He sweeps everything from his desk. He picks up a chair and smashes it into a cabinet. He thrashes and flails around, smashing up the whole room until all his anger, upset and frustration are spent. **Arthur** *cowers in the corner, not moving. This is* **Makepeace***'s gig. He sits numb at his ruined desk.*

After time to gather himself, he picks up the phone and dials a number. As he is calling, **Kitty** *slowly walks from the dock, along the street and up the steps to the office.*

Makepeace   Hello. Taylor, please. Taylor – the insurer. Hello . . . Yes. Yes . . . The *Good Hope* . . . They found a hatch. And a sailor . . . What's that . . . no, we're not surprised either. What are the odds after sixty-odd days . . . yes, that's right . . . never a pleasant business . . . yes, I'll wait for you at my office. Thank you . . . Goodbye.

Kitty *comes in. She stands still at the door.* **Makepeace** *has his back to her and doesn't see she's there.*

Kitty   . . . I . . .

Eventually, the door falls shut, with a slam, as **Makepeace** *turns . . .*

Makepeace   Can't you knock?

He sees **Kitty** *and freezes.*

Kitty   I . . .

Makepeace   You're too late. They've gone.

He looks at her.

Kitty   Is it true . . . is it true . . . ?

Makepeace *looks at her.* **Kitty** *collapses.* **Makepeace** *runs to her and cradles her.*

Makepeace   Kitty. Kitty. Damn this awful business.

Arthur   Shall I get a doctor, sir?

Makepeace   No. Stay where you are. She's coming round.

Kitty *sobs for a long time in* **Makepeace**'s *arms.*

Arthur   Mrs Fitz . . .

Makepeace   Let her cry.

Makepeace *pushes* **Arthur** *away. He holds her tightly as she cries. It is an intensely personal moment between them.* **Makepeace** *is holding on to her for dear life.*

Kitty   He didn't even want to go. I had to prise him off t' doorpost.

Makepeace   You did nothing wrong.

Kitty   And I put on his dad's earrings – like a lamb to the slaughter.

Makepeace   Sssshh. Shh.

Kitty   And I never even saw my eldest go –

Makepeace (*deeply moved*)   Please. Stop.

Kitty   You know he could've been yours.

Makepeace   I'm sorry, Kitty.

Kitty   He might have been yours.

Makepeace   O God, I wish it were different.

Kitty   You loved me, Christopher.

Makepeace   It were a long time ago, Kitty.

Enter **Clementine**. *She looks in horror at the destruction.*

Kitty   You loved me.

Clementine   Kitty.

Kitty   Four sons. And a husband.

Clementine   Please, don't worry about anything. I've set up an appeal. It will be in the papers tomorrow. Arthur. (*She gives him a sheet of paper.*)

Makepeace *gestures for* **Clementine** *to leave.* **Clementine** *takes no notice and tends to* **Kitty**.

Clementine   Please, Dad, let me stay with her. I'll bring some hot soup. And you must come back to clean for us. You won't object, Dad? We'll look after you. Really.

Clementine *leaves hurriedly.*

Kitty   My only hope is James's bairn.

Makepeace   Bairn?

Kitty   Another accident. Jo.

She laughs.

Accident? It's no accident . . .

Makepeace   Please, you mustn't tell anyone about this. Please, it's for your own good. You know the rules of the fund, Kitty. You know they won't pay up with bastards in the house.

Kitty   Is that how you see it?

Makepeace   Kitty. It's nowt to do with me. You know that committee. Please, think about this. Your son in jail – your niece. I'll do my best but for God's sake don't mention this yet . . . there are seven families – sixteen orphans.

He stands and paces around.

Oh, Kitty.

Kitty   Is that all you can say.

Clementine *has arrived at the door with some hot soup. She is holding it in both hands and calls to* **Arthur** *to open the door.*

Clementine   Arthur. Arthur.

Arthur *opens the door and* **Clementine** *comes in with the tureen of soup.* **Makepeace** *stands at one end of the room, unable to say anything.* **Kitty** *is at the other frozen.* **Clementine** *goes to* **Kitty**.

Clementine (*very gently*)   Here.

Kitty *doesn't respond.*

Clementine   If you don't want it here – take it home. You can bring the bowl back whenever.

Kitty *stares ahead.* **Clementine** *puts the dish into her inanimate hands. A pause.* **Kitty** *is motionless with pain. She carefully puts down the tureen and walks out of the office. We hear her footfalls as she walks away. It is a long, devastating walk through the town, through the sails.* **Makepeace**'s *office disappears and she is alone walking through the endless sails, slowly getting smaller. We hear the footfall of clogs echo as she makes her lonely, proud walk down the quay until she is a tiny figure in the vast distance. She descends the steps down to the fish dock and disappears.*

The stage is empty. Distant voices quietly singing. The snow stops falling.

Epilogue

Spring 1901.

The snow miraculously disappears. It is a bright spring morning. The tattered sails of winter seem brand new and flapping resplendently in the breeze. From the back of the stage we hear a chorus of voices stridently singing.

Chorus
    Raise your banners high
    Strength to strength and line by line
    Unity must never die
    Raise your banners high.

Slowly, from the rear of the stage the townsfolk march forward in unison across the stage. In the centre, leading the progress is

Makepeace *with* **Clementine** *close to his side. They move as one towards the audience, resolute and hopeful.*

Raise your banners high
Strength to strength and line by line

They reach the very front of the stage. The line stretches from wing to wing. The entire community, except the men lost during the play, are gathered in an ensemble that echoes the opening image. They sing with strength and purpose.

Unity must never die
Raise your banners high.

As the anthem comes to its natural conclusion **Makepeace** *turns and through the crowd he brings* **Kitty** *carrying a wreath bearing the legend: 'The Good Hope'.* **Kitty** *throws it into the pit/the sea. The tableau freezes. A huge flash as if from a camera.*

Blackout.